David Clarke

Scared to DEATH

And other ghost stories from Victorian Sheffield

Acknowledgements

I wish to thank The British Library for permission to use images from the Charles Dickens exhibition, 'A Hankering after Ghosts' and from the 19th Century British Library Newspapers website, copyright The British Library Board. The cover image of Campo Lane and images from Picture Sheffield are used with the permission of Sheffield City Libraries and Archives. I wish to thank Sheffield City Council/Registry Office for their assistance in obtaining the death certificates on pages 21 and 86. Thanks to Fortean Times/ David Newton for permission to use the image on pgs 16-17. In addition I wish to thank Ann for her patience during the design and production process, Carolyn for proof-reading, Vanessa and Alan for their testimonials and Neil for taking on the project. Every effort has been made to trace owners of copyright material. Any omissions will be corrected in later editions. Please contact the author at **furnival.news@googlemail.com**

ISBN 978-1-908431-22-6

Published by ACM Retro Ltd.
Registered office:
51 Clarkegrove Road
Sheffield S10 2NH

Visit us at www.acmretro.com

Layout and design by Ann Beedham.
Photos and illustrations by Ann Beedham unless stated

Cover photo: Campo Lane, Sheffield Sheffield Libraries

Bunting Nook, a well known
'haunted site' in Sheffield

Preface

In this fascinating book, distinguished folklorist and historian David Clarke reveals the rich ghostly heritage of Sheffield. He has done exactly what every good researcher should do, going back to the earliest sources, to explore a city and its environs which abound with supernatural stories and folklore. In doing so, he has recovered numerous accounts which have languished for far too long between the pages of Victorian newspapers, magazines and journals. Whether you believe ghosts are real or not, they certainly exist as social facts in Sheffield life, with each of the stories being expertly examined here in terms of their historical, folkloric and cultural meaning and significance.

Sheffield Cathedral
- where the Gabriel
Hounds passed over

Despite a long-standing prejudice entertained by many folklorists – itself Victorian - that industrial centres were bereft of ghostlore, such stories and beliefs positively flourished in cities such as Sheffield throughout the 19th and 20th centuries. Many of these apparitions were considered remarkably solid and malevolent, leaving tangible traces such as footprints, and creating real panic in their wake. Like many other places across England, Sheffield suffered visitations from the infamous 'Spring Heeled Jack', and its skies were pierced by the cries of aerial phantom dogs, the Gabriel hounds.

But Sheffield also possessed a unique collection of localised phantoms, including a variety of shape-changing goblins, boggards and barghasts such as 'Tom Dockin' or 'Tom Rawhead" and troublesome spectres such as long-running Campo Lane Ghost. Whilst some such stories were considered simply a device for scaring wayward children, it is obvious that many of the adult population readily believed in the reality of these supernatural entities, with named witnesses being cited for them and certain houses readily identified as being frightfully haunted.

Indeed, so strong was the belief in ghosts that tragic consequences could follow, both the community and for individuals. Nowhere is this more highlighted than with the strange case of Hannah Rallison, a 48 year-old woman sensationally reported as 'Frightened to death by a ghost' in 1855. Yet, despite a well-publicised death being attributed to nervous shock occasioned by a ghost, as David Clarke demonstrates it did nothing to deter many people from seeking a personal supernatural encounter of their own. Whole crowds might go hunting the ghosts rumoured to prowl their communities, whilst individuals and families willingly invited spirits into their homes to manifest at spiritualist séances.

On occasion, some people even resorted to posing as ghosts, attracting the attention of the police and magistrates as a result of their antics.

Thus, whether you are approaching the ghosts of Sheffield from a passion for history and learning about the lives and beliefs of our forebears, as a researcher probing the mysteries of the paranormal, or simply from a wish to be entertained like generations before us by a thrilling ghost story suitable for Christmas, you will find *Scared to Death and other ghost stories from Victorian Sheffield* a most valuable and absorbing book, and one which will be enjoyed for many years to come.

Alan Murdie,
Chair, The Ghost Club, August 2013

Contents

PRICE ONE SHILLING.

A WONDERFUL GHOST STORY
Being
Mr H's Own Narrative
A RECITAL OF FACTS
With Unpublished Letters
FROM
CHARLES DICKENS
Respecting it

GRIFFITH & FARRAN, LONDON.

A Wonderful Ghost Story published in
London, 1882 British Library Board

Paradise Square, Sheffield, close to
where a woman was 'scared to death'

Introduction

'...as the night lengthens, and the days shorten, the ghosts gain in strength and reach their highest at Yule time.'

Collected in South Yorkshire by S.O.Addy 1895

Of the many inventions inherited from our Victorian ancestors, the Christmas ghost story must be one of the finest. People have told stories about restless spirits and other supernatural beings from time immemorial, but it was not until the 19th century that the first elaborate 'ghost stories' began to appear in print.

The most famous of all is Charles Dickens' *A Christmas Carol*, but his most realistic ghost story, *The Signalman*, was written in the aftermath of his narrow escape from death in the Staplehurst rail crash of 1865. The eerie setting, in a dark, grim railway tunnel, was filled with the same dread and foreboding that was felt by many of his contemporaries who feared new technology. *The Signalman* was, according to Matthew Sweet, the literary embodiment of Victorian anxieties about train travel and 'about the ghosts in the machine of the industrial revolution'.

Charles Dickens,
1812-1870
British Library Board

Two decades earlier, as he worked on *A Christmas Carol*, Dickens drew upon older traditions and beliefs about purposeful ghosts. The four redemptive spirits that visit Ebenezer Scrooge at midnight on Christmas Eve – a magical time in folklore - were meant to torment well-to-do members of Victorian society. Early in the story, Scrooge rebuffs a request for a donation to help the poor who, at the time of its writing in 1843, were caught in a prolonged period of depression and unemployment. 'Are there no prisons?', is Scrooge's retort, 'And the Union workhouses...are they still in operation?'.

Before long he is confronted with the ghost of his dead partner Marley, 'dragging chains...made of cash-boxes, keys, padlocks, ledgers, deeds and heavy purses wrought in steel'. Even then he refuses to believe the evidence of his own eyes, blaming the apparition on 'an undigested bit of beef, a blot of mustard, a crumb of cheese'. But his skepticism evaporates during the journey that follows. Whisked through time and space, accompanied by the spirits of Christmas, he revisits his own past and witnesses the tribulations of the Cratchit family and their ailing youngest son, Tiny Tim.

The Spirit of Christmas Present introduces Scrooge to two more children, hidden beneath his cloak; a boy and girl 'meagre, ragged, scowling, wolfish... where angels might have sat enthroned, devils lurked'. Scrooge asks if they belong to the spirit, who responds: 'This boy is Ignorance. This girl is Want. Beware them both...but most of all beware the boy, for on his brow I see that written which is doom'. When a troubled Scrooge asks why they have no refuge or resources, the spirit quotes his own selfish words: 'Are there no prisons?...Are there no workhouses?'.

Dickens' visits to the ragged schools introduced him to street children who lived in destitution within one of the wealthiest cities in the world. He was determined to use his story to improve their condition. For his biographer Clare Tomalin, this was the true highlight of the story, 'as Dickens sends a resounding message to the governing powers of his day'. Its power to tap into the collective conscience may explain why the message of *A Christmas Carol* continues to find resonance in audiences today.

HENRY TATTON

In writing this book I have leaned heavily upon the writings of earlier authorities who recognised the important role played by folklore in the social and religious history of Sheffield and its surrounding area. One local author who influenced the direction of my research is Henry Tatton. He was born in Sheaf Gardens, Heeley, in 1861, close to the home of my great-grandparents who, like many Sheffielders at that time, earned a living as cutlers. At that time Heeley was a rural village with fewer than 2000 inhabitants but times were changing. By 1881 the population had swelled to 9000 and by 1911 this had doubled again. The small cottages, farms and cutlers' workshops that were familiar to Tatton in childhood were being swept away by the demands of heavy industry. Sheffield was being transformed into a modern city. For half a century, Tatton ran an ironmonger's stall in Sheffield Market but in 1920, at the age of 59, he decided to learn how to draw. Soon he began sketching the characters and buildings that he remembered from what he called 'old Sheffield'.

Tatton also kept voluminous hand-written notes on local history and folklore and contributed to *The Sheffield Independent.* Eventually this collection swelled into three volumes of manuscript notes. His jottings include references to the ubiquitous legends of underground passages linking Heeley with the Manor and Sheffield Castle. He also mentioned famous ghosts that haunted the streets and alleys of Victorian Sheffield, including 'Spring-heeled Jack', the spirit rapper of Pearl Street and the apparition that appeared in George Street in 1882. In a note dated 1934 he refers to other haunted houses 'in Fountains Square, where Martin Street is now [in Upperthorpe], and they could not get anyone to live in it, and another near Weston Park that was supposed to be haunted'. His manuscript, *Sheffield*, can be consulted at Sheffield Local Studies library. Henry Tatton died in 1946.

Marley's ghost
visits Scrooge
British Library

Ghost stories played an educational, as well as a moral function, in Victorian society. For instance the invocation of bogeymen, both real and supernatural, to scare misbehaved children, is a recurring theme in folklore. Elsewhere, terrifying ogres and assorted monsters from myth and legend were employed to deter young children from dangers lurking in dark alleyways, ponds and rivers. So while some skeptical members of Victorian society maintained that ghost beliefs were dying out in the face of technological progress, the cumulative evidence suggests the opposite. Mass ghost-hunting expeditions to 'haunted houses' became a popular form of entertainment for the British working classes in urban areas like Sheffield. The spontaneous gathering of hundreds, sometimes thousands, of curious onlookers outside haunted buildings was a Victorian phenomenon. The historian Owen Davies has studied newspaper reports of ghost panics from this period. He discovered that '...word of mouth obviously spread quickly in urban neighbourhoods [but] like... other working-class festive events, the authorities and the press saw ghost hunts as uncouth and vulgar, a disgraceful mix of "superstition" and lack of civility'.

Individual participants, when quizzed by journalists, confessed they were acting on information supplied by word-of-mouth or, increasingly, sensational reports in newspapers and periodicals. News travelled faster as technology improved the means of production and distribution. From 1855, when the stamp tax was abolished, more people could afford to buy newspapers and within months 17 regional titles were created in England, including *The Sheffield Telegraph,* the town's first daily paper. With the passing of the Education Act in 1870 the numbers of literate people grew and so did the demand for literature of all kinds.

This was reflected in the popularity of the Victorian equivalent of today's tabloids, *The Illustrated Police News*, whilst the Penny Dreadfuls catered for the public's insatiable demand for crime, adventure and scandal. Popular literature transformed Victorian bogeymen Spring-heeled Jack, Sweeney Todd and Jack the Ripper into legends, while the fascination with ghosts and other supernatural horrors was catered for by the theatre and the fairground. Ghost Shows were a semi-permanent feature of the many travelling fairs that, from the early 19th century, featured thrilling attractions such as the 'hobgoblinscope'.

As the stories featured in this book illustrate, ghost alarms were a common pastime in the streets of Sheffield, and indeed many other towns and cities, during the Victorian era. Those fascinated by ghosts were a cross-section of working class and artisan society, but the majority, according to Owen Davies, and 'often the catalysts for ghost hunts' were boys and young men. The youthful composition of the crowds may reflect the universal desire of young people to experience the vicarious thrill provided by fear of the unknown that, to this day, draws viewers to horror films and inspires others to dress up as ghosts and ghouls on Halloween. Virginia Woolf pondered on 'the strange human craving for the pleasure of feeling afraid which is so much involved in our love of ghost stories'. She decided that it was 'pleasant to be afraid when we are conscious that we are in no kind of danger'.

As remains the case today, Victorian society was divided between those who expressed belief in ghosts and the skeptics who dismissed all supernatural phenomena as humbug. The Victorian elite blamed 'superstition' and ignorance as the source of many ghost beliefs. Scientists and rationalists explained ghost experiences as optical illusions, or hallucinations resulting from over-indulgence, as in the undigested 'piece of cheese' referred to by Scrooge.

Charles Dickens maintained a skeptical attitude towards the supernatural but nevertheless, as one of his biographers, John Forster, noted, he retained 'something of a hankering' towards ghost stories and he continued to return to the subject.

Like Dickens, from an early age I have had 'a hankering after ghosts' and, like him, I have always believed that supernatural manifestations must have a rational explanation. That conviction has been constantly challenged during the three decades in which I have gathered the materials for this and other books.

So when people ask me 'do I believe in ghosts' my response is to sit on the fence. For the record, I do not believe in the existence of ghosts as the restless souls of dead people, who return to Earth like Jacob Marley, to execute some mission or to right some wrong. I prefer the more nuanced view of that master of ghost storytelling, M.R. James, who was born during the Victorian era. In his autobiography, published in 1936, James referred to the existence of 'sequested places', here and there, where: '...curious creatures still frequent, whom once upon a time anybody could see, whereas now only at rare intervals does one cross their path and become aware of them; and perhaps that is just as well'.

SYDNEY OLDALL ADDY (1848 - 1933)

The Folklore Society was founded in 1878 and its members began to collect and record local traditions, customs and belief. Included within its remit were supernatural beliefs and experiences. One of the society's most enthusiastic members was a Sheffielder, Sidney Oldall Addy, who was born in January 1848 at Cole Aston and educated at Sheffield Collegiate School and Lincoln College, Oxford. Addy's parents wanted him to become a priest but he chose law and began practising as a solicitor in 1877. His true passion, however, was folklore and one contemporary described him as 'a solicitor by profession but an antiquarian by instinct'.

Sydney Oldall Addy
Sheffield Libraries

He immersed himself in ecclesiastical history, folklore and architecture and wrote frequent letters to the local *Notes and Queries*. He served ten years as president of the Hunter Archaeological Society and published his first major work, *Historical Memorials of Beauchief Abbey*, in 1878.

During Addy's lifetime steel-making overtook cutlery as the most important industry and the increasing demands for skilled workers led to mass migration from the surrounding countryside. Sheffield was transformed within the space of sixty years from a collection of semi-rural villages into a bustling metropolis, with its skies choked with smoke and its rivers polluted with the products of heavy industry.

It was during this time of rapid and sometimes violent change that Addy set out to record fragile items of local dialect, place-names, traditions and beliefs. Many of these are lost today, so his writings have become doubly important to social historians. In the foreword to a reprint of *Household Tales with other Traditional Remains* (originally published in 1895), Professor John Widdowson writes that Addy 'either wrote down the tales from dictation or was given a written copy of them' by his informants. He did not succumb to the temptation of polishing or modifying them and most important of all, they were collected from the oral tradition. His informants were ordinary people, including some who had settled in Sheffield from areas as widely separated as North Yorkshire, Lincolnshire and Ireland. Describing the traditions he collected, Addy wrote that 'many more of them must be embedded in the memories of the people, but the collection of these things usually falls to the lot of those who are otherwise busy'.

Like other Victorian folklorists, Addy believed that some old traditions were inherited from pre-Christian beliefs held by Anglo-Saxons and Scandinavians who settled this region during the Dark Ages. He detected traces of archaic pagan beliefs in rhymes and sayings, folk tales and, most prominently, in place-names. ▶

SYDNEY OLDALL ADDY (continued)

Both the introduction to Addy's glossary of local words and a chapter in his book *The Hall of Waltheof* (1893), subtitled 'or the early condition and settlement of Hallamshire', were dedicated to divining the pagan or mythological origin of local place-names.

In his *Glossary of words used in the neighbourhood of Sheffield* (published in 1888), Addy refers to a note by an earlier historian, Joseph Hunter, concerning the name of the principal river of Hallamshire. Although universally written as Don in modern times it was once referred to as the Dun, perhaps from the Celtic word for 'dark'. Hunter added that 'in common talk' Dun rhymed with son as in a sinister old saw:

The shelving, slimy river Dun,
Each year a daughter or a son.

Hunter was unaware of the river being 'infamous for accidents of the type alluded to' but Addy, who was familiar with similar traditions associated with the River Spey and Dart, disagreed. He 'had no doubt that these lines point back to a time when human sacrifices were offered to the god or goddess of the river'.

In *The Hall of Waltheof* Addy mentions the existence of a medieval chapel of Our Lady on the bridge that crosses the Don between Waingate and the Wicker, that still retains the name of Lady's Bridge. There is a similar chapel on the Don in Rotherham town centre. He posed this question to the reader: was the worship of 'Our Lady' at these chapels in medieval times 'merely the substitution of a Christian saint for a pagan god or goddess of the river?'.

Addy was not the only local historian to speculate about the survival of ancient beliefs in folklore and place-names. In his memoir *A Life at One Living*, the Rev Alfred Gatty, vicar of St Mary's Church, Ecclesfield, told of a visit he made in 1884 to The Canyards, a group of 'curious shaped mounds and hillocks of the most fantastic character' near the prehistoric Bar Dyke earthwork at Bradfield. A friend of Gatty's believed the place-name dweorgadenu, recorded in Dwarriden farm and Dwarriden Lane, close to the hills, was of Anglo-Saxon or Scandinavian origin, and meant 'the valley of the dwarfs'. Gatty continues:

'...he begged me to go there and see if there was any peculiar echo, as the Norse term for echo was "the voice of the dwarfs". I paid a visit to the spot in the spring of this year, just when the larches were putting out their fairy-like buds of green; and these, with the darker foliaged Scots firs and pines, growing among these strange mounds and hills, made the scene resemble some abode of elves. I shouted, and echoes on all sides answered me; some horned sheep, scared by the sounds, scampered away among the rocks, and an old cock grouse rose on the wing, crowing lustily'.

Belief in the existence of a race of dwarfs, who lived in rocks or beneath hills where they excelled in metalworking, continues today in Iceland. Early English traditions of this kind were immortalised in J.R. Tolkien's *The Lord of the Rings.*

AUTHOR'S NOTE ON SOURCES

Scared to Death is my attempt to combine ghost stories, items of folklore and personal experiences in one collection based around the ghosts that preoccupied Sheffielders during the reign of Queen Victoria.

My interest in the supernatural began in childhood when my grandparents entertained me with memories of their lives in early 20th century Sheffield. Their accounts of survival through two world wars were lightened by tales of local characters, criminals and bogeyman such as Spring-heeled Jack and the 'King of Burglars', Charlie Peace. They learned of the latter from their own from parents and grand-parents, whilst

Charlie Peace in 1878
South Yorkshire Police

the former continued to live on in the collective memory of their generation (see pg 55). Exposure to this rich collection of lore, that stretched back two generations to the late Victorian period, inspired me to begin collecting stories and legends.

Until the arrival of the internet, newspapers and magazines were an unrivalled source of news, correspondence and debate on the subject of ghosts and other mysteries. During my time as a journalist at the *Sheffield Star,* I came to appreciate the important role newspapers played as a conduit whereby ordinary people could talk freely about their extraordinary experiences with ghosts and other strange phenomena.

During the 1990s I interviewed dozens of people who rang or wrote to *The Star* describing their own ghost experiences and *The Star's* records were supplemented by a larger collection of stories held by Sheffield Local Studies Library and Archives. This included thousands of books, pamphlets and memoirs, many out of print. But as no indexes of content were available for most regional newspapers, until recently research into their content was a laborious process.

These problems were resolved in 2007 when The British Library launched the 19th century newspaper project. This had two objectives. Firstly, to preserve the originals for the enjoyment of future generations and secondly, to make thousands of pages available online. Now, via the British Library's website, it is possible to search newspapers electronically from the comfort of your armchair. This new technology, made available via the internet, would have seemed like magic to a journalist working in Queen Victoria's reign.

Fortunately for me, the entire 19th century run of *The Star's* predecessor, *The Sheffield Telegraph,* and that of its main rival, the *Sheffield & Rotherham Independent,* were included in the British Library project.

The research I conducted on these two daily newspapers forms the core of the stories recounted in *Scared to Death.* It is complimented by extracts from the writings of my predecessors as chroniclers of Sheffield folklore, such as Sidney Addy and Henry Tatton, alongside material I have collected during the course of more than a quarter of century hunting for ghosts in the archives and libraries of the city.

MEETING GHOSTS

What may be the oldest recorded ghost story from Sheffield is dated 26 June 1688. It comes from an authoritative source, being part of a collection of depositions collected by magistrates at the Castle of York and reads:

'John Bowman, of Greenhill, co. Darby, taylor, saith, that upon the Tuesday before Ascension Day last, hee was comeing home from Sheffield market on the footway towards Highley [Heeley]; and about the midway there was one John Brumhead overtook him, and they past along until they came against the cutlers bridge. And when they came at the said bridge they had some discourse concerneing an apparition that had been seene there, as it was reported, in the shape and corporall forme of a man that they called Earle George. And as they were speakeinge of itt, of a sudden there visibly appeared unto them a man lyke unto a prince with a greene doublet and ruff, and holding a brachete [hound] in his hand. Whereupon this examinate was sorelye affrighted and fell into a swound or trance, and continued in the same, as hee conceiveth, for the space aboute halfe an houre. And when he awakend he saw a man passinge with two loadend horses, and he went with him towards Highley'.

The 'Earl George' who appeared to Bowman – causing such shock that he lost consciousness - must be the Lord of the Manor, George Talbot, who was 6th Earl of Shrewsbury and the third husband of Bess of Hardwick. The Earl was the reluctant gaoler of Mary Queen of Scots

during her imprisonment in Sheffield in the reign of Queen Elizabeth I. In total Mary was held prisoner for 14 years at Sheffield Castle and the Earl's residence at Manor Lodge before her execution for treason. On his death in 1591 the Earl was buried in an elaborate tomb in the Shrewsbury Chapel of Sheffield's parish church. After his death traditions about Mary's imprisonment continued to circulate in the town, including the persistent belief that she was moved around in secret via a network of underground tunnels linking the castle with the Manor Lodge and other locations in the town centre.

George Talbot
Sheffield Libraries

Bowman's account suggests that he was aware of stories about the Earl's ghost haunting the bridge at Heeley, or 'Highley' as it was known at that time. The connection between Heeley Bridge and Earl George is unclear, but ghosts often lurked under bridges or deep within pools and water-sources. In folklore these, like subterranean tunnels, were often regarded as portals between this world and the otherworld.

Detailed first-person accounts of ghost experiences such as Bowman's are rarely found in written records before the 19th century. Before that time, collectors of folklore tended to concentrate on traditions and folktales that were often disparagingly referred to as 'old wives tales'. Sidney Addy's method of collecting was somewhat unusual in that he recorded both traditional stories and personal experiences such as this story:

Norton parish church

'about 1840 the parish clerk of Norton, in Derbyshire, and his apprentice went to play the organ, then standing in the west gallery of the church. The apprentice, whose face was turned towards the nave of the church, told the clerk he could a see a woman sitting alone in one of the high cloth-covered pews, and that he believed she was spectral. Thereupon they both rushed frantically down the steps, which were very tortuous and awkward. The clerk would never again play the organ in church in the dusk of evening'.

Addy was born in the parish of Norton and his account contains such a level of circumstantial detail that it is likely he heard it either directly from the clerk himself, or second hand from a relative or acquaintance.

Today the mass media is a plentiful source of direct eye-witness accounts of ghost experiences. Newspapers and magazines regularly carry detailed first-person accounts of hauntings and the views expressed by those who believe and disbelieve in ghosts. In contrast, stories published by Victorian newspapers appear long-winded, with reportage mixed up with the personal opinion of the writer, who more often than not expressed disapproval. Even worse, the style of Victorian journalism often contained overt prejudice towards foreigners, women and members of the 'lower orders of society' that would not be acceptable to a modern readership.

Following the abolition of stamp tax in 1855 many new regional newspapers appeared to cater for a growing readership. Fair and accurate reporting of local news became an important priority for editors, as did the publication of a wider range of stories from Victorian society. First-hand accounts of ghost experiences began to appear in newspapers towards the end of the Victorian era, usually in the form of correspondence from readers. For example, in a letter published in 1882, 'a Sheffield gentleman' told how, 'the other night, when walking up a well-lighted street, I saw a woman in front of me at about 100 yards distance. As I drew nearer, I was struck by her indefiniteness of outline and want of solidity'. His wonder grew when a horse-drawn cab crossed the end of the darkened street. The outline of the cab could be plainly seen through the intervening figure.

Finally, the diaphanous woman 'glided slowly across the pavement and vanished apparently through the solid wall'. Despite the extraordinary nature of this experience, the letter-writer refused to completely believe the evidence of his own eyes. In his account he felt obliged to reassure readers that he had consumed only coffee during the day and 'neither was my imagination excited by alcohol as I am a total abstainer'. Immediately doubters sought to find a rational explanation for his encounter. One commentator suggested that 'some practical joker with a magic lantern produced the illusion from a neighbouring window'.

1
SCARED TO
DEATH...

'That popular belief in ghosts is not extinct, even in a large town like Sheffield, is proved by [these] tragic circumstances...we leave it to the ingenious reader to explain away these appearances – fancied or real – upon rational grounds. We content ourselves with 'telling the tale as 'twas told to us,' satisfied that we have detailed for public delectation a ghost story which is far too good to remain hidden in obscurity.'

On 3 March 1855, under the headline 'FRIGHTENED TO DEATH BY A GHOST', Henry Pawson, editor of the *Sheffield Times*, announced that '...this ghost story is one of the prettiest we have heard for some time.... It has appeared to three persons. The first it alarmed; the second it threw into fits; and third it killed. What more can be needed to convince the most skeptical?'

The ghost's victim was 48-year-old Hannah Rallison. She was the wife of labourer John Rallison and they rented a room in the Park district of the town.

A year before her own death, the couple's eldest son died in a Sheffield colliery accident. Both Hannah and John were members of a new religious movement, the Church of Latter Day Saints or Mormons. According to contemporary newspaper accounts, a short time before her death Hannah Rallison was introduced by a fellow Mormon, John Favell, to a young widow, Harriet Ward.

A writer in the *Sheffield & Rotherham Independent* said of Ward: '...of all the young women we have come in contact with for many a day, not one appears to us so likely to see a ghost as Ward, about whose appearance and demeanour there is a wildness indicative of an uncommon exuberance of imagination'.

When in February 1855 Favell, along with his wife and her sister, rented a tenement in Campo Lane, they brought Ward with them as a lodger. The property occupied by the Favell family, near the present-day corner of Campo Lane and Church Lane, consisted of a first floor shop and a cellar kitchen. The 1851 census lists a Harriet Ward, aged 27, as the wife of George Ward, shopkeeper, on Eldon Street.

According to the *Sheffield Times*, by 1855 Ward was a widow, but she claimed to have received frequent visitations from her husband's ghost.

Image: Fortean Times /
David Newton

She had converted to Mormonism after a brief flirtation with spiritualism, both religions being recent arrivals from America. Ward had attended some of the first spiritualist sittings in the town, presumably in an attempt to contact the spirit of her late husband, and was present at a séance when 'spirit rappings' were heard.

Immediately on moving into Campo Lane the Favells were disturbed during the night by 'strange sounds which might have their origin in supernatural agency', but the family 'set it down as the effects of the imagination'. Nevertheless they grew so fearful that none would venture downstairs into the cellar kitchen after dark.

Then, at midnight on Saturday 24 February, Harriet Ward entered the cellar on an errand. A loud scream was heard and the Favells rushed downstairs to find her leaning against a table, her features rigid and her eyes fixed upon a point in the room where she claimed a ghost could be seen. The Favells told her they could see nothing. Ward fainted and on her recovery she described the apparition as 'a grim-featured old woman wearing a long white nightgown and a full-bordered cap'.

Ward saw this apparition on five occasions during the next 24 hours whilst awake, and whilst asleep in her dreams.

Campo Lane in the 19th century
Photo: Sheffield Library Archives

In one vivid dream the woman in white led her to 'a purse of gold', buried under the flagstones of the cellar floor, whereupon her landlord John Favell took out the purse and said: 'That's all we want, let the old ghost come now'. Buried treasure guarded by ghosts was a common theme in English folklore and this type of story would have been familiar to many in the surrounding countryside.

Campo Lane
Photo: Sheffield
Library Archives

Ward's visions continued on the Sunday, when John and Hannah Rallison and their landlady, Mrs Johnson, visited to lunch with the Favells. During the meal, Ward declared she could see the ghost on the cellar steps. On this occasion the apparition displayed bloodstains on its face and neck. Her screams brought John Favell running down the cellar steps, at which point his feet 'appeared to touch the ghost's head'. But he saw nothing 'as the superstition runs that only a few people are gifted with the power to see ghosts'. Ward said the apparition appeared to disappear in the same corner of the cellar kitchen where her dream had indicated treasure lay hidden.

On Sunday afternoon, 25 February, Favell, Rallison and Ward attended a church meeting at the Mormon Hall of Science, where the Campo Lane ghost was the main topic of conversation. Later that evening a larger group of friends, including church elders, returned to Favell's residence. By now the spirit pointing to buried treasure had been transformed into a vengeful ghost who had returned to reveal the last resting place of a murder victim. As a journalist remarked: 'of course, there could be no ghost without a murder...and therefore all the gossips have declared that the white lady's aim is to obtain a Christian burial and bring to justice, if still living, the perpetrators of the crime'.

The wild claim that treasure, or the body of a murder victim, lay beneath the floor of his cellar kitchen led John Favell to remove heavy stone flagstones from the floor of the cellar. Outside in Campo Lane, a crowd began to gather. What happened next was described in proceedings of the inquest held on 27 February in the Mason's Arms public house at South Street in the Park district. It was presided over by Sheffield deputy coroner, Henry Badger. The jury was told that as midnight approached a group of two dozen people, including Harriet Ward, along with the Favells and the Rallisons were present in the first floor of the tenement. Annoyed by the crowd growing outside, Mrs Favell asked her sister to cover the window of the cellar with a blind. Fearing what she might see on the cellar steps, she hesitated.

At this point Hannah Rallison took the blind and went downstairs, accompanied by her landlady, Mrs Johnson. After fixing it she turned around to face the cellar steps and was immediately paralysed with fear. According to *The Sheffield & Rotherham Independent* account Hannah fainted but regained consciousness for a brief interval during which she said 'she had seen a female form dressed in white, on the stairs; that it seemed to approach her suddenly, became a substance without form, and vanished as it rushed past her'.

A SHEFFIELD " GHOST."

Unfortunately for Spiritualism, there have been many ghost stories prior to the interesting narrative told by the Sisters Fox, and one of the best authenticated of modern times is that which has found a permanent abiding place in Sheffield archives under the name, if we are rightly informed, of the Campo-lane Ghost. " Once upon a time" a certain house in Sheffield had an evil reputation for being haunted. Tenant after tenant would have it that " Old Nick " had set up his mansion in that particular dwelling, his favourite place of resort being—save the mark—in the cellar! This latter circumstance did not seem greatly to redound to his Satanic Majesty's good taste, but the fact was sworn to, nevertheless, by several witnesses that a hobgoblin of some description had been repeatedly seen capering on the whitewashed wall of the humble vault referred to. The civic authorities were appealed to, and the custodians of the public peace were set on watch, but all in vain. The "ghost' could not be "apprehended." At length the despairing landlord offered a reward of £5 for any hardy wight who would be bold enough to beard the spirit in his ... other ... ...

As friends and relatives attempted to revive the unconscious woman in the first floor room, Harriet Ward announced that she could see the ghost of the white lady at the top of the stairs. She claimed the apparition opened its white night-dress to reveal deep gashes in its neck and blood-stains. Ward challenged the ghost in the name of the Father, Son and Holy Ghost to say why it troubled her. In Sidney Addy's collection of folklore the following advice is given to those who are confronted by a restless spirit: 'If a ghost appears, and you say to it, "In the name of the Lord, why visitest thou me?" it will tell you what it has come for'.

On this occasion, the ghost did not respond to the challenge but beckoned for Ward to follow it. Gripped by 'some irresistible urge', she descended the steps while Favell, 'struck by her wild, terrified, appearance,' took hold of her arm, and followed. Ward said the ghost again disappeared into the corner of the cellar kitchen.

That was far from the end of the story. At this point, according to newspaper accounts, Ward began to communicate telepathically with a spirit that only she could see. She demanded to know 'Why do you trouble me?' and this time received an answer, although not an audible one. The white lady produced a sheet of spirit paper on which the words 'I am murdered' appeared. Ward asked: 'By whom?' and as more questions spilled out of her mouth, words materialised on the paper, 'the letters of one answer fading as another made its appearance'. For a period of one hour, Ward dictated the full detail of her telepathic conversation as the Mormon elders copied the words down. The spirit told her it was the restless soul of Elizabeth Johnson, murdered by her nephew, William Dawson, on 26 March 1722 and buried deep beneath the cellar 'in a watery grave'.

The final message was: 'The garret and the cellar are now marked with my blood. You must quit this house, because William [Dawson] will trouble you if you don't'.

The séance ended with the sudden disappearance of the ghost, 'whereupon [Ward] fainted and remained insensible for about a quarter of an hour'.

Hannah RALLISON	Female	48 years	Wife of Robert Rallison Labourer	Sudden death in a fit beleived to have been brought on by fright

Hannah Rallison's
death certificate
Sheffield Registry Office

Meanwhile, upstairs, Hannah Rallison was removed from the premises in a horse-drawn cab. She was taken to her home where she died the following afternoon. At the inquest the jury questioned a number of those who were present at Campo Lane but 'could not make anything of the ghost story' and returned a verdict of death through natural causes. Rallison was described by the coroner as 'a strong, healthy woman, labouring under no disease as far as is known' but he concluded her death had 'certainly been caused by the fright she had received on the previous day, up to which time she was in perfect health and spirits'. Hannah's death certificate, held by Sheffield City Registry Office, records the cause as '...sudden death in a fit believed to have been brought on by fright'.

FRIGHTENED TO DEATH BY A GHOST.—That the popular belief in ghosts is not extinct, even in a large town like Sheffield, is proved by a tragic circumstance of recent occurrence. It was currently reported in Campo-lane, at the latter end of last week, that a ghost, "all in white," had made its appearance in the house of John Favell, who lives in Campo-lane, a little beyond the parish church. The story was genuine thus far, that a young woman named Harriet Ward, who lodged at Favell's house, affirmed in the most solemn manner that she had seen an apparition in the cellar-kitchen. This assertion was made with such an air of credibility that the other inmates of the house—Favell, his wife, and the wife's sister—could not altogether disbelieve it, though they had no visual evidence of its truth. Favell had heard strange sounds, however, which he thought might have their origin in supernatural agency. On Saturday evening they felt so much concerned on account of the ghostly presence that for the sake of greater security a friend of the family, a man named Robert Rollinson, who lodges in Court No. 24, South-street, Park, was requested to spend the night at Favell's house. Being neither superstitious nor timid, Rollinson acquiesced. He and the other persons

The death of Hannah Rallison was the final straw for the Favell family. Along with the occupants of four neighbouring properties, they abandoned the haunted tenement and moved to another rented dwelling nearby.

On the evening of Tuesday 6 March 1855 a crowd of three hundred people gathered on Campo Lane, blocking movement on the road outside. Windows were broken, lead was stolen from the roof and an outhouse demolished. *The Sheffield Times* reported the haunted properties belonged to a landlord, Mr Levy, of High Street, 'and has already been damaged by mischievous persons among the lookers-on, and the police have experienced great difficulty in preventing destruction on a much larger scale. That enterprising body of individuals, the pickpockets -who loose no opportunity, whether grave or gay, of pursuing their vacation – have been busy among the crowd in Campo Lane. Mrs Jackson, a furniture broker, living near the "haunted house", was standing at her door talking to some friends...when her pocket was picked of 30s, a bunch of keys and some other articles of small value'.

During the mayhem, another group of 'roughs', their courage fuelled by drink, broke into the property and began hauling up flagstones from the cellar, in search of the buried treasure. Several bystanders were violently robbed and a force of six policemen were called for. As they tried to clear the road, the mood grew angry and two constables were left injured in the street battle that followed.

The editors of *The Sheffield Free Press* and *Sheffield & Rotherham Independent* expressed outrage at the scenes of disorder and violence on Campo Lane. They declared they did not believe in ghosts and did not want to see property damaged and law abiding people robbed or assaulted by those who did. Both were scathing in their criticism of what they called 'the Campo Lane delusion' and heaped the blame for the mayhem upon 'credulous Mormonites'.

And there was one final bizarre twist in the tale. On 17 March 1855 *The Sheffield Independent* published a scathing report that appeared to point the finger of blame for Hannah Rallison's death at Ward and her 'hysterical hallucinations'. But on another page it declared the sensation was not entirely the product of the imagination after all: 'We have been informed that some of the alleged appearances have resulted from operations with a magic lantern by the occupiers of adjacent premises, who knew that Favell and his family were Mormonites, and determined to have a lark at their expense.'

Insinuations of credulity were frequently levelled at members of dissenting congregations and Methodists, for example, were mocked for being gullible because of their interest in supernatural phenomena. So it was natural for debunkers of ghost stories to suggest the Mormons had been duped by pranksters. In later years, the magic lantern explanation was adopted, at least by the literate residents of Sheffield, as a satisfactory explanation for the Campo Lane ghost. Two decades later, a writer in *The Sheffield Telegraph* referred to 'the evil spirit' as having 'turned out...to be nothing more nor less than the shadow projected by a magic lantern on the white-washed cellar wall'.

Journalists who interviewed those concerned at the time remained convinced that something uncanny had occurred in the house on Campo Lane. A representative of *The Sheffield Free Press* recounted how 'the parties concerned in this affair, whom we have seen solemnly affirm its truth, and as solemnly believe that it is the work of a supernatural agency'.

It also reported that John Favell continued to believe a woman had been murdered in the house during an earlier century. He would not be dissuaded from this certainty when a journalist informed him the rented tenement he had vacated had been constructed two decades earlier.

A number of accounts mention a variety of colourful rumours that were current in the town, 'one is that the ghost had appeared to a watchman, and so terrified him that it had been necessary to take him to the Infirmary; another that a man (unknown) had been carried away in a fit, and declared to be in a dying state by Mr Wood, surgeon; a third that the bones of a human being had been found beneath the cellar kitchen floor'.

A fourth rumour in circulation claimed the landlord of the haunted house, now vacant, had offered a sovereign 'to any individual who would spend a night in the place.' *The Sheffield Times* said this story attracted thrill-seekers from outside the town including 'a stolid-faced gentleman in a smock-frock and a hat with an extensive brim'. He appeared at noon one day among the crowd in Campo Lane 'and employed himself in making inquiries about "t'chap what was willing to give a pound for somebody to sleep in t'house what was t'ghost was"...after some time fruitlessly spent in seeking out a person who was willing to give the sovereign, and endeavouring to strike a bargain with the neighbours to sleep in the house for a less sum – he went down as a low as eighteen-pence, it is stated – the disappointed countryman wended his way home, a wiser and sadder man'.

The story about the landlord's wager enjoyed such longevity that it became the Victorian equivalent of an urban legend. It turns up in a summary of the Campo Lane story, published by a Coventry newspaper on Halloween 1876.

In this version the white lady ghost has been substituted with Old Nick himself.

'...several witnesses had sworn that a hobgoblin of some description had been repeatedly seen capering on the whitewashed wall of the humble vault. The civic authorities were appealed to, and the custodians of the public peace were set on watch, but all in vain. The ghost could not be apprehended. At length the despairing landlord offered a reward of £5 for any hardy person who would be bold enough to beard the spirit in his den, otherwise cellar. A taker was eventually located for the wager, 'who undertook, provided his natural courage was supplemented by a liberal administration of that other courage known as "Dutch" to lie in wait for the evil sprite. When the news got wind, an immense concourse of people collected in the adjacent street, for the Campo Lane ghost had by this time acquired a Sheffield-wide celebrity, and the result of the daring experiment was awaited with intense excitement. All went well till the mystic time of night arrived when churchyards yawn, but no sooner had the town-bells tolled the solemn hour of twelve than a sudden shriek was heard in the silent house, a basement window was abruptly thrown open, and out leaped, in frantic horror, the hardy watcher, with the terrible exclamation on his lips: "the devil"....'

Some God-fearing Sheffielders remained convinced the Campo Lane ghost was an evil spirit or demon sent by the Devil. Sidney Addy's collection of folklore, published in 1895, refers to a tradition that: '...the Devil is always in our midst at twelve o'clock, the hour of midnight', and the superstitious could not ignore the fact that the Campo Lane ghost appeared at the 'witching hour'.

These fears may have been increased in March, 1855, when *The Sheffield Times* published further news of strange hoof-like footprints in the winter snow at Loxley Common (see p 31). Was Old Nick stalking the winter landscape looking for souls to steal away? Certainly the community of Mormons caught up in the Campo Lane mystery appeared to believe this was the case. Soon after the inquest verdict on Hannah Rallison the *Sheffield Independent* reported that Harriet Ward, the only person to whom the ghost had shown itself apart from its victim, had been excommunicated by a unanimous vote of the Mormon congregation. They had decided 'the apparition... emanated from his Satanic majesty, and hint that wonderful things may be expected in these marvellous times.'

BARGHASTS AND BOGGARDS

Campo Lane had an eerie reputation long before the sensational events of 1855. Early drawings and photographs show rows of tall stone properties lining the thoroughfare, adjacent to the north side of Sheffield's parish church (now Sheffield Cathedral).

Journalist John Holland described hearing those harbingers of calamity, the Gabriel Hounds, whilst passing through the darkened churchyard one dark night in 1861 (see 'The Sky Yelpers', p38).

Old, boarded up properties often became the focus of ghost rumours. Joseph Woolhouse, writing in 1832 as the cholera epidemic took its toll on the city's inhabitants, told of 'a large stone house [that was] untenanted a many years when I was a boy because say'd report in those days it was haunted and no one durst live in it (what a dark age).'

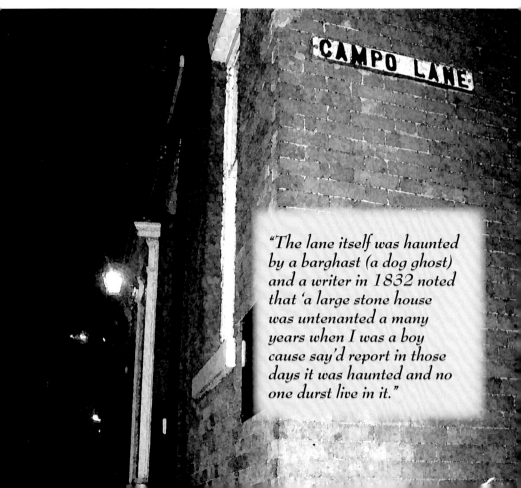

"The lane itself was haunted by a barghast (a dog ghost) and a writer in 1832 noted that 'a large stone house was untenanted a many years when I was a boy cause say'd report in those days it was haunted and no one durst live in it."

This appears to be the same large, unoccupied house at Hawley Croft mentioned by Joseph Hunter in his book *Sheffield in the Eighteenth Century.* Hunter said in his day the 'haunted house' sported a 1721 datestone and Woolhouse said this building later became tenanted as the Ball Inn at 26 Campo Lane. Thomas Hinchliffe, writing in 1879, mentions yet another haunted house on the same lane. This was distinctive in having 'two old fashioned shop bow-windows' and a 1742 datestone. At the time of writing it was 'unoccupied and in a dilapidated condition' even though it was 'the largest and best house in Hawley croft'.

The Ball Inn, 26 Campo Lane
Photo: Sheffield Library Archives

The most elaborate ghost story associated with Campo Lane before the mid-19th century was the tale of the barghast. Woolhouse's account of this goblin is set in the 17th century and came to him second-hand via an employee of his grandfather who made pocket knives and kept a public house in Green Lane, near Paradise Square:

'One of his men was lame and compell 'd to have crutches to assist him to travel for a number of years. His residence was in Gregory Row...This person was out late one evening and had to come on Campo Lane, he saw (or fancied he saw) the Bargast (as it has been frequently called) coming towards him on Campo Lane. At that time the Paradise Square was a field and a Stile at the top to go over.

'When he first saw this goblin he thought within himself "If I can but get over this stile into the field I can go down the hill merrily". Gregory Row was a very narrow row or street at the bottom of Paradise Square. This was a very high hill at that time. The bottom of the present street has been raised 3 or 4 feet in my time. He managed over this stile, but the fiend gained ground on him. Faster he went and faster it followed, he ran with his crutches till his fears came thicker and faster, and this demon still getting nearer, when, being about the middle of this field (the Square) seeing this goblin close at his heels, he there dropt his crutches and away went he without them, and never stopt or look'd behind him until he got home (he lived in Gregory Row, a very narrow thoroughfare out of West Bar Green and came out at the bottom of Silver Street at the back of the now Sign of the Little Tankard). The wife had the door made, but him being in such a fright had not patience to wait until she opened the door but burst it open. He told the wife what was at the door, but she was the worse frightened at him coming without his crutches than at the Bargast. However they were a little reconciled and went to bed. He could not rest from fright etc., got up at daylight to go in quest of his crutches; he found them in exactly the same place where he dropt them. He went to his work the next morning and his Shopmen was nearly as frightened to see him come trotting to the shop without his crutches as he was when he saw the Bargast. However he was so overjoyed that he gave his shopmen a treat of some ale, and they spent the day cheerfully; and he for his own part never used crutches again while he lived, and he lived a many years after this'.

While Woolhouse's informant does not describe the 'bargast', it is a familiar 'bogey-beast' in the nomenclature of British goblins. The Oxford English Dictionary defines the barghaist or bar-ghost (pronounced ba-gest) – from the German bier-ghost - as 'a goblin, fabled to appear in the form of a large dog, with various horrible characteristics'. Meeting the barghast was meant to 'portend imminent death or misfortune' which explains the fear experienced by Woolhouse's informant. But in his case, the encounter had a happy ending in that he is apparently cured of his lameness.

Joseph Hunter's *Hallamshire Glossary* describes the barghast as a shape-changing apparition that sometimes resembled a dwarf human being; at others it appeared as a large dog-like animal. It was definitely a town ghost '...seen at the corners of streets or near half-broken walls, with his long teeth and saucer eyes, the only feature by which he is distinguished.'

In Hunter's time the barghast was used 'to alarm naughty children into order and obedience'; when a schoolboy in Attercliffe 'we had rumours of its appearance not far from our playground, but I never saw it and suppose that if anyone did see it he was deceived by a trick played by persons in those days, which consisted of placing a candle within a hollow turnip, in the rind of which holes were cut, through which the light appeared'.

Sidney Addy described the barghast as 'a being which resembles a large, black dog, having eyes like saucers'. One appeared in a children's playground at 'The Brocco', on the steep hill between Solly Street and Allen Street, Netherthorpe, in 1828, but this turned out to be a hoax. A more ominous example was seen by a woman at 'three lane ends' at Bury Hill, near Holmesfield. It was invisible to her sister who died one month later. According to Addy: 'If you see a barghast it will be visible to your companions if you touch them'.

A creature called Tom Dockin was a fearsome barghast whose name was used to instill fear in Victorian children. In a letter published by *The Sheffield & Rotherham*

Independent (3 December 1888) John Wilson said he asked an old woman of 90 years if she had heard of this creature. 'She at once said children were told "if they were not good Tom Dockin would fetch them". He was a frightful bogey to children [and] was sometimes described as having iron teeth with which he devoured bad ones'.

Sidney Addy, in his *Supplement to the Sheffield Glossary*, says Tom Dockin was 'well known as a goblin about Sheffield' and compared Dockin with a Norse word dockalfar, 'or dark elves, who dwell down in the Earth'. The same or a similar goblin was known as Tommy Raw-head, Tom of the Wood or Raw-head-and-bloody-bones. At one time parents would warn restive children, 'tha moant go out at neet, or Tommy Raw-head will fetch thee'. According to Addy, a spring or well at Hackenthorpe was called Tommy Raw-head Well by children because they believed 'an iron man with chains on his body' lived beneath it.

The boggard or boggart was a related spectre, 'a local goblin or sprite said to haunt a particular gloomy spot or scene of violence', often a dark place in a country area away from the territory of the town-ghost or barghast. There was a phrase 'to take boggard' used in the South Yorkshire region. This meant to 'take fright'. The Thorpe Hesley Boggard in Rotherham was said to be the ghost of the 1st Earl of Strafford, Thomas Wentworth. He was a key advisor to King Charles I during the English Civil War and was condemned to death by Parliament. Strafford was beheaded in 1641 on Tower Hill after the king signed his death warrant and his body was buried in secret at Hooton Roberts, near Rotherham. It is said that at certain times his restless spirit walks down Haigh Lane from Wentworth carrying his head under his arm. He is also said to wander the oak-panelled corridors of the family seat at Wentworth Woodhouse. The appearance of Strafford's boggard may have given rise to the saying, once prevalent in the district: 'That comes and tha goes like the Thorpe Hesley Boggard!'

The sign at Boggard Lane, Oughtibridge

Boggard Lane at Oughtibridge first appears on Ordnance Survey maps of Bradfield parish, Sheffield, in 1891. There is no written record of a ghost in Boggard Lane but local historian Malcolm Nunn says he has heard 'several stories in that area of unusual happenings in recent times'.

Today the long, tree-lined track is interrupted by a spring and overlooks a cemetery and chapel at its western end. As night fell, those travelling along this rural lane in times past could be forgiven for quickening their pace whether or not they believed in ghosts and boggards.

Perhaps the best known Hallamshire boggard was that haunting Bunting Nook, in the parish of Norton. This goblin was familiar to Sidney Addy who was born in the parish in 1848 and recalled 'the boggard of Bunting Nook' being 'held up as a terror to children'. The lane, which runs along the eastern edge of Graves Park, was 'a dark, umbrageous place' in Victorian times. Three roads met there and Addy noted that crossroads were often said to be 'haunted by barghasts, boggards, or headless women'.

Today Bunting Nook retains is eerie reputation. Local author Valerie Salim, in her 1983 book *The Ghost Hunter's Guide to Sheffield*, records a number of legends about the lane. She says: 'the only time I've had any eerie sensations myself was walking there' but adds that she had 'read so much about it, and of the green human-shaped mists that people see there, that your imagination can run riot'.

Bunting Nook, Norton

BUNTING NOOK
8

Scared To Death

MYSTERIOUS FOOTPRINTS AT LOXLEY.—Mysterious footprints, such as were first seen a couple of months ago in Devonshire, aud a *fac-simile* of which appeared in the *Illustrated London News,* have been seen at Loxley near this town—on the lawn in front of Loxley cottage, the residence of Mr. Blackwell, solicitor. The like singular impressions, if impressions they are, were noticed for the first time by Mr. and Mrs. Blackwell in the snow which covered the ground about the middle of January, and were seen again towards the end of that month. They corresponded exactly to the engraving in the *Illustrated News.* Yesterday morning the snow on Mr. Blackwell's lawn presented identically the same unexplained appearances. There were two separate tracks at a distance from each other, and as to one of them there was this singular characteristic—the line terminated abruptly at each end, without communicating with any other footmarks. Supposing, then, that the marks were the impressions of an animal's feet the animal must have dropped as it were from the clouds, run a few yards upon the snow, and again taken wing. The suggestion that the footmarks are those of a badger does not apply, therefore, in this case. They were not footprints at all, in fact, for the snow was not rendered additionally dense as it would have been if subjected to pressure. It has been suggested to us that the strange appearances may be the result of some atmospheric phenomenon at present not understood.

Footprints in
the snow
Daily Express

2
THE DEVIL'S FOOTPRINTS

In 1855 Queen Victoria was beginning the seventeenth year of her long reign and the British Empire was at war in the Crimea. At home the country was gripped by the most severe winter within living memory. In January the rivers Trent, Severn and Exe froze and heavy snowfall followed. Against the backdrop of this winter landscape, one of Britain's most perplexing unsolved mysteries, the Devil's Footprints, was written. On the morning of 9 February 1855, residents of towns across southern Devon awoke to marvel at what *The [London] Times* called 'An Extraordinary Occurrence'.

In the snow, mysterious hoof-like marks were found over a distance of 40 miles, on both sides of the River Exe, as if 'some strange and mysterious animal endowed with the power of ubiquity' had created them during the night. The single line of tracks resembled those of a donkey, but spacing between impressions suggested they were made by someone walking upright on cloven feet.

The account published by *The Times* told of hoof-prints 'seen in all kinds of inaccessible places - on tops of houses and narrow walls, in gardens and courtyards enclosed by high walls and palings, as well as in open fields. There was hardly a garden in Lympstone where the footprints were not observed. The track appeared more like that of a biped than a quadruped, and the steps were generally eight inches in advance of each other'.

There were many explanations for the tracks. Badgers, otters, kangaroos, birds, rodents and even a balloon trailing a horseshoe-shaped grappling rope were all suggested by assorted experts. A sketch of the prints was published by *The Illustrated London News* in a report that summarised the popular theories, adding: 'At present no satisfactory solution has been given. No known animal could have traversed this extent of country in one night, besides having to cross an estuary of the sea two miles broad. Neither does any known animal walk in a line of single footsteps, not even a man'.

If the maker of the footprints was not an animal or a man, then what was it?

Comic book illustration of Devil's Footprints
Target Magazine, 1972

Superstitious people believed they were the work of the devil himself and in the Devonshire villages they were referred to as 'The Devil's Walk'. At the time readers of the accounts in London newspapers believed the phenomenon were unique to the West Country, but earlier in the winter similar mysterious footprints appeared in other parts of England and Scotland.

A cluster of strange footprints was found at Loxley, near Sheffield. It was here, early in January, again after a snowfall, that solicitor George Henry Blackwell and his wife Margaret noticed a series of peculiar marks in the garden of their cottage adjacent to Wadsley and Loxley Commons. Interviewed in March by *The Sheffield Times,* Blackwell said the tracks 'corresponded exactly to the engraving in *The Illustrated London News*' of the Devonshire footprints. He added they appeared for a second time before the end of January, more than a fortnight before the phenomenon was first mentioned in the national press. The footprints were in the form of two separate tracks spaced at a distance from each other. 'As to one of them there was this singular characteristic - the line terminated abruptly at each end, without communicating with any other footmarks,' Blackwell said. 'Supposing, then, the marks were the impressions of an animal's feet the animal must have dropped as it were from the clouds, run a few yards upon the snow, and again taken wing'.

To Blackwell, a suggestion by a naturalist that the Devonshire tracks were made by a badger was nonsense [because] 'they were not footmarks at all, in fact, for the snow was rendered additionally dense as it would have been if subjected to pressure'. The editor of *The Sheffield Times* said it had 'been suggested that us that the strange appearances may be the result of some atmospheric phenomenon at present not understood'.

If some 'atmospheric phenomenon' really was responsible for the prints it would have to account for more than just a singular appearance. Strangely, Loxley Common already had an existing tradition concerning supernatural footprints that

Was this the cottage where the 'devil's footprints were found at Loxley, near Sheffield ?

appear in the winter snows. An account of the Loxley footprints appears in an evocative ghost-story, attributed to a local writer who signed himself 'J.T.H'.

I first came across an account of the 'Legend of Loxley Common' in J. Edward Vicker's book *Old Sheffield Town*, published in 1972 and it has since appeared in many other publications. The source is a story published by the *Sheffield Independent* shortly before Hallowe'en in 1912, and this is worth reproducing in full:

GHOST OF LOXLEY CAVE
Weird Story of two New Year Eves of Long Ago

The sun had set full early that day, and storm clouds lowered. At the lonely cottage on Loxley Common a mother croodled over her sleeping babe, listening eagerly for the steps of her husband - Lomas Revill, gamekeeper to the Lord of the Manor. He ought to have been home long before that. It was a weary vigil, the monotony of which was relieved only by a caller from the hillside. And when she had gone the mother watched the flickering, uncanny shadows cast by the log fire until she grew weary [of] watching, and dreaming, and wondering.

Struggling fitfully, the moon sought to pierce the heavy, snow-laden clouds; but the wind howled fiercely and the storm king reigned supreme.

Benighted natives coming from Worrall to Loxley casually sought shelter from the wintry blast and ere the storm was at its height left the tired mother alone with her sleeping babe. The hours passed, and the storm raged more furiously and swept the blinding snow until the common was shrouded in a thick mantle of white.

Footprints in the Snow

It was New Year's Eve, a century ago, when morning broke an acquaintance from the adjacent hamlet of Wadsley called to exchange the compliments of the day with the dwellers at the lonely cottage. She knocked hard at the door, again and again, but there came no response. She tried the latch, which had not been dropped, and walked in.

The young mother lay there dead - murdered! But the babe in the cradle slept on. Outside, the great world was clad in white. The snow had drifted into little mountains all along the heath and amongst the crags which form a rough boundary between the Loxley Common and Wadsley Common. There was no trace of life or activity save in one direction. Right across the ridge and on the open common were footprints, huge footprints, as if a man had travelled that way; but, unhappily the drifted snow had partly obliterated them and here and there they were quite lost. But the strange footprints were distinctly traceable to 'the cave' - really an ancient cave-like well - on the crown of the hill overlooking the valley. There they ended, or began. There was slight evidence of blood and washing in the water. The footprints were distinctly to the cave, walked into it, walked round it and were lost.

Strangest of all, so the tale of the Common goes, there was nothing to show that the maker of the footprints had passed to and from the well; except that the huge footprints might have been made by the traveller tramping back from the spot in his own footsteps. But the drifted snow made the theory problematical. Maybe, the man, for man it seemed to be, had taken refuge in the cave-well while the storm raged and so his first footprints were lost.

Mystery of Tragedy

When news of the crime was posted to the neighbouring hamlets there was much weird speculation and superstition. What was the mystery of the footprints at the cave? The tragic story was conveyed to the keeper at his cabin in the woods. He accepted it with little show of surprise, and no emotion. He had been seen at the village inn the night before much the worse for drink, and none could swear that he had not spent the night in the cabin.

The moorland murder was a mystery indeed, and for years the good folk fought shy of Loxley cave when the shadows of night had lowered. And it was observed that Lomas Revill became a strange man, prematurely aged, and his hair turned white at 42. Another New Year's Day came.

Once more the countryside was a foot deep in snow. Lomas Revill had been missing for some days from the post of duty at his cabin in the wood, and when the searchers led them to the outbuildings of the cottage on the Common they found him there, hanging from a rafter - dead.

Why should Lomas Revill do this? Beneath his cabin locker were found buried a hunter's knife, rusted in gore, and a pair of blood-stained gaiters. People did say that Revill was often strange when that particular season came round, and he often muttered that he 'could stand it no longer'.

Beyond these slender clues there was nothing to connect the gamekeeper with the murder of his wife; but suspicion had clung that way.

Wall O'er Moor, Crag and Heath

Superstition seized the simple, homely folk of the countryside. When storm clouds frowned, and when the snow whistled in the wind over the common and the pale moonlight cast its haunting shadows on crag and heath, so 'twas said, the ghost of Mary Revill walked abroad plain for all folk to see. Of fancy pictures and stories there was no lack. Wanderers over the common and lanes about thought of Frank Fearn's gibbet, which creaked in the wind on Loxley Edge merely a stone's throw away, and all but the stout-hearted were 'feared' to pass that way o'nights lest they should encounter the ghost of the wailing mother and her sleeping babe. Should you travel that way even now perchance you may meet some veteran who will tell you a snatch of a story of a strange murder and two suicides. Perhaps he will tell you also that certain other cottages on the common stand ruined and derelict simply because most people were 'feared' of ghosts which were said to haunt these parts.

Thus runs the weird story of the ghosts of Loxley Common, which may be revivified by the feeling which haunts the wanderer who loiters on the common after dark. Old folk still recall bad cases of garotting on the Common, and other tragic things associated with the now ruined and lonely cottages at the end of Loxley Common. Hence it comes that mystery, fact, and superstition crowd in upon each other when the weird story of that old-time New Year's Eve is retold.

The 'cave well' mentioned is the Cave House said to have been built by a Unitarian minister, Thomas Halliday, as part of his plan to attract tourists to the area that became known as 'Little Matlock'. He died in the 1830s and the Cave House itself is believed to date from the mid-18th century. The fire-proof structure was demolished in the 1920s but would have been a familiar landmark when this story appeared in *The Independent*.

As part of his plan to attract visitors to the area Halliday purchased empty land on the common where the body of Frank Fearn had once been displayed, hanging from a gibbet post. In 1782 Fearn was convicted at York Assizes of the robbery and murder of a watchmaker Nathan Andrews, on the Kirk Edge Road. The sentence was death but, following the custom of those violent times, that was not sufficient to atone for the crime and a deterrent was required for others.

Therefore his body was to be gibbeted on Loxley Common near the scene of his crime.

Fearn's bones fell from the post in 1797 and, significantly, the presence of his grisly remains on the gibbet is mentioned in the legend of the common. Although the post itself was removed in the early years of the 19th century, rumours about restless spirits haunting the common remained in circulation throughout the Victorian period. They were still current nearly two centuries later when I collected stories and experiences in the area. Feelings of 'intense fear' at certain locations and eerie noises, as if from the clanking of a chain against the gibbet post, have been reported by residents.

His body was to be gibbeted 'on some conspicuous spot' on Loxley Common near the scene of his crime. Fearn's bones fell from the post in 1797 and, significantly, the presence of his grisly remains in the gibbet is mentioned in the legend of the common

Loxley Common, near the site of Frank Fearn's gibbet

Loxley and Wadsley Common has long associations with outlaws. A record of the estates of Thomas Howard, Earl of Arundel, refers to the foundations of a house called Little Haggas Croft in Loxley Firth that was pointed out, in 1637, as the place where Robin Hood was born. Ten years after Fearn's body was gibbetted it became the place of refuge sought by John Oxley, an accomplice of the highwayman Spence Broughton. Oxley committed suicide on the Common rather than face the fate of Broughton who was gibbetted on Attercliffe Common (see page 100). His demise must have added to the eerie reputation of the area that continues today.

Legends are stories about actual people, places or strange events that are told as if they were true. Clearly people once believed that Mary and Lomas Revill were real people and that Mary was murdered and her husband was found hanging from the rafters of their cottage. Unfortunately, research has found no evidence that anyone called Revill lived or died in the vicinity of the Cave House. More conclusively, there appears to be no record of a murder or suicide on Loxley Common in the circumstances described by the legend.

So were the Revills real people or just legendary characters like that other famous resident of Loxley, Robin Hood? Was the legend of the Common simply a piece of imaginative fiction presented as fact? Or was it a mixture of traditions connected with Fearn's gibbet and existing ghost beliefs?

The Devil's Footprints that appeared on the Common in 1855 suggests there was a tradition about demonic happenings at Loxley that may have inspired the description of the mysterious footprints leading to the Cave House, used to good effect in the story. And if my theory is correct, the story of Mary Revill's murder might have provided an enterprising local story-teller with material that would nicely explain sightings of a white lady ghost on Loxley and Wadsley Commons. For in January 1920, the same newspaper that published the legend, *The Sheffield*

...all but the stout-hearted were 'feared' to pass that way o'nights lest they should encounter the ghost of the wailing mother and her sleeping babe.

Independent, told of a sensation created in Worrall and Loxley by the appearance of 'a woman in white who glides silently and now and again raises her arms in lament or imprecations'.

The lane from the field road to Bradfield, site of a ghost encounter
Photo by the author

This ghost was said to haunt Long Lane, near the old ganister mines, and, according to the newspaper, 'some people claim she occasionally moans as if in trouble. Folk who claim to have encountered the ghost state it walks abroad between the hours of 9 and 11 o'nights'. A reporter located one eye-witness, a labourer called Clarence Swain. He had been walking towards the city with his sister late on the evening of 31 January when, 'making our way for Hillsborough we saw it. When we got against the lane end that comes from the field road to Bradfield, she clutched at my arm and, upset-like, screamed 'Oh look Clar!', and when I looked there was something white coming across, like a woman, maybe, holding her arms up. Then it vanished across by the old pit. It scared me right, and my sister couldn't talk for a bit, as she was very feared'. Responding to the journalist's suggestion that they might have been nervous in the darkness, Swain said: 'Me nervous? I was never feared before of man or spirits, but if that wasn't a spirit, I'm beat'.

'Or a white cow?' asked the reporter.

'Cows don't glide over walls,' he replied.

The strange happenings had been the centre of gossip at the bars of the Blue Ball and Shoulder of Mutton but 'without [anyone] being able to explain why the ghost was supposed to be a woman'. If the story of Mary Revill's murder on Loxley Common was as well known as the legend published eight years earlier implied, why would the identity of the ghostly woman in white be so contentious?

A follow-up report in the *Independent* said that hundreds of people, many from the city centre, had since journeyed to Loxley Common at night to take part in 'ghost hunting'. 'Much amusement has been aroused and, among the villagers of these lonely parts, not a little misgiving [although] several more residents in Wadsley and Worrall declare they have seen the strange visitor'.

Today people continue to see the White Lady of Wadsley Common. In January 1985 two girls on horseback saw 'a young girl in a long dress' run across the snowy ground in front of them and vanish into thin air. Their horses were terrified and remained restive when they returned to the stable.

The account does not mention if the ghost left a trail of footprints in the fresh snow...

3
SKY YELPERS
THE GABRIEL HOUNDS

'Curse the Gabriel hounds! It is the first time I have spoken of them
since that awful night; it is the last time I ever will speak of them.
What they are, God, who made them, knows.
Only I pray I may never hear them again,
nor any friend of mine.'

Sheffield Cathedral, the former
parish church, where John Holland
thought he heard the Sky Yelpers

Sky Yelpers

"They staggered and stumbled on, not now with any hope of extracting themselves from Cairnhope Peak, but merely to keep the blood alive in their veins. And, when they were exhausted, they sat down and soon were heaps of snow. While they sat thus, side by side, thinking no more of love, or any other thing but this - should they ever see the sun rise, or sit by a fireside again? Suddenly they heard a sound in the air behind them, and, in a moment, what seemed a pack of hounds in full cry passed close over their heads. They uttered a loud cry.

'We are saved!' cried Grace. 'Mr Raby is hunting us with his dogs'.

'That was the echo,' Coventry groaned. 'What scent would lie?' said he. 'Those hounds were in the air, a hundred strong'. Neither spoke for a moment, and then it was Grace who broke the terrible silence ---

'THE GABRIEL HOUNDS... The Gabriel hounds that run before calamity! Mr Coventry, there's nothing to be done now, but to make our peace with God. For you are a dead man, and I'm a dead woman'. She kneeled down in the snow, and prayed patiently, and prepared to deliver up her innocent soul to Him who gave it'.

This scene appears in Charles Reade's novel *Put Yourself in His Place*, published in 1870. His tale is unique in painting a vivid picture of life and death in mid-Victorian Sheffield: '...an infernal city, whose water is blacking, and whose air is coal'. In the novel Sheffield, then still a town, is referred to as Hillsborough and much of the narrative is based around the notorious Trade Union outrages of the 1860s. Reade cleverly weaves supernatural elements into the plot that draws its characters into a dramatic conclusion during greatest peace time disaster in British history – the Sheffield Flood of 1864.

The journalist Samuel Harrison described the deluge as 'a calamity, appalling and almost unparalleled' in his *Complete History of the Great Flood at Sheffield*. Between 250 and 300 people died when the embankment of the newly-built Dale Dyke Dam at Bradfield, northwest of the city, burst just after midnight on 12 March 1864. Millions of gallons of water spilled into the valleys of the Loxley and Don within half an hour, washing away houses and people. Many of the victims found themselves trapped inside buildings caught in the path of the floodwaters.

After the waters retreated, human and animal bodies were found washed up by the debris 15 miles along the valley towards Rotherham. Some victims were never identified.

Those who lost their lives, many of whom were children, received no advance warning of their watery fate. But one story recounted in Harrison's book tells of a 'remarkable dream' that saved seven members of the Ibbotson family caught in the path of the floodwaters at Bradfield.

Mr Richard Ibbotson 'rescued five of his children to a place of safely some hours before the flood came,' Harrison explained. 'His house was flooded, and he had to

Flood damage at Neeepsend, Sheffield in 1864 Photo: Sheffield Libraries

carry his wife and child in blankets to the house of his brother. On the night before the flood his wife had a very peculiar dream. She dreamt that she was in a flood, and that she had a very narrow bridge to cross, but with great difficulty she managed to get across. It was in consequence of this dream that five children were removed before the flood came. Mr Ibbotson says that his clock stopped at two minutes past twelve, and that, as the clock was right to a minute, that was the time of the flood'.

We will never know how many other 'peculiar dreams' and premonitions were experienced by those caught up in the great Sheffield flood. The account in Reade's book is preceded by a sense of impending doom, heightened by the appearance of a pack of spectral hounds that pursue and fascinate the heroine, Grace Carden.

In one scene Grace and Mr Coventry are warned about the hounds by the squire, Mr Raby, who says he has never seen a ghost but has heard one. 'Whether it was supernatural I can't say, but, at least it was unaccountable and terrible,' he said. Asked to explain what the Gabriel hounds are, he replies:

'A strange thing in the air, that is said, in these parts, to fortell calamity'.

Traditions of a phantom huntsman and hounds hunting lost souls across the skies are common in English folk traditions. In Devonshire, the huntsman who leads the demonic Wish Hounds across Dartmoor on stormy nights is identified as the Devil himself. In other parts of the country the huntsman is the archangel Gabriel, who is sometimes referred to as the angel of death. A Derbyshire correspondent of *Notes & Queries* wrote in 1886 of the uncanny sounds as 'the angel Gabriel hunting...[the damned] and...the cries were uttered as the lash of angel's whip urged them along'.

Charles Reade drew upon South Yorkshire traditions about the Sky Yelpers for his novel. His contemporary, Sheffield folklorist Sidney Addy, refers to Gabriel Hounds as 'a peculiar noise in the air' associated with death and calamity.

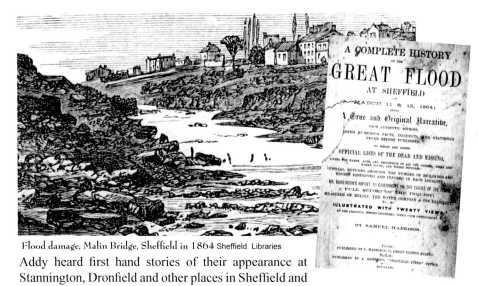

Flood damage, Malin Bridge, Sheffield in 1864 Sheffield Libraries

Addy heard first hand stories of their appearance at Stannington, Dronfield and other places in Sheffield and Derbyshire, and he noted a tradition that 'when a storm sweeps over Ringinglow, near Sheffield, people say that Michael and his dogs are passing over'.

In Reade's book, pressed by Grace Carden to describe the 'Sky Yelpers', Mr Raby says: 'Well, one night I was at Hillsborough on business and as I walked by the old parish church, a great pack of beagles, in full cry, passed close over my head... they startled me, as I never was startled in my life before. I had never heard of the Gabriel hounds then, and I was stupefied. I think I leaned against the wall there before I recovered myself, and went on'.

But what did this supernatural vision mean?

'You shall judge for yourself. I had left a certain house about an hour and a half: there was trouble in that house, but only of a pecuniary kind. To tell the truth, I came back with some money for them, or rather, I should say, with the promise of it. I found the wife in a swoon; and, upstairs, her husband lay dead by his own hand'. At this point Raby stands and paces arout the room in an agitated state, exclaiming: 'Curse the Gabriel hounds! It is the first time I have spoken of them since that awful night; it is the last time I ever will speak of them. What they are, God, who made them, knows. Only I pray I may never hear them again, nor any friend of mine'.

Next morning Grace asks a servant woman, Jael Dence, if she had ever heard of the hounds. At first she looks puzzled but then says: 'Why, that would be Gabble Retchet. I wouldn't talk much about the like, if I were you, miss'.

But Grace persists and extracts an admission that Sheffielders often heard sounds in the air, like a pack of hounds in full cry. These always warned of death or disaster but '...they are not hounds at all; they are the souls of unbaptized children, wandering in the air till the day of judgement'.

One of Reade's sources was the Tyneside-born poet and folklorist William Henderson, who had many friends in South Yorkshire. His book *Notes on the Folk-Lore of the Northern Counties* was published in 1866, two years after the Sheffield flood. Henderson says in Durham and parts of Yorkshire the Gabriel Hounds themselves were believed to be not lost souls but monstrous human-headed dogs who move through the air and are often heard but seldom seen. In Reade's novel Jael Dence refers to them as Gabble Retchet and the phrase *gabrielle rache*, first recorded in 1483, simply means 'corpse-hound'. This may refer to the old superstition that dogs could sense the presence of spirits and would howl as a prelude to a death.

Henderson says an informant '[tells] me that when a child was burned to death in Sheffield a few years ago, the neighbours immediately called to mind how the Gabriel hounds had passed above the house not long before'. Another source told him of a person hastily summoned one night to the sick-bed of relative whose condition had suddenly deteriorated. 'As he set out he heard the wild sound of the creatures above his head; they accompanied him the whole way, about a mile, then paused, and yelped loudly over the house. He entered it, and found that the patient had just breathed her last'.

HOUNDS OVER SHEFFIELD

Mr Raby's dramatic encounter with the Gabriel hounds near 'the old parish church' is based upon a real experience described by one of Sheffield's most famous Victorian journalists, John Holland. Born in the Park district in 1794, Holland was a prolific poet and author who succeeded his friend and fellow radical, James Montgomery, as editor of the *The Sheffield Iris* newspaper.

In a letter dated 28 March 1861, quoted in Henderson's book, Holland said he could 'never forget the impression made upon my own mind when once arrested by the cry

Alley at the side of Sheffield Cathedral

of these Gabriel hounds as I passed the parish church of Sheffield, one densely dark and very still night. The sound was exactly like the questing of a dozen beagles on the foot of a race, but not so loud, and highly suggestive of ideas of the supernatural'.

Holland tried to rationalise his eerie experience in an article for *The Sheffield Telegraph* in 1869. Once a large flock of wild migrating geese alighted at the north side of the church, startling the sexton, he said, and 'perhaps the nocturnal "yelp" of the so-called "Gabriel Hounds" is due to birds of this class'. Nevertheless, Holland wrote a sonnet based upon his own and others' experiences of the Sky Yelpers.

Sky Yelpers

Oft have I heard my honoured mother say,
How she has listened to the Gabriel hounds
Those strange unearthly and mysterious sounds.
Which on the ear through murkiest darkness fell;
And how, entranced by superstitious spell,
The trembling villager not seldom heard.
In the quaint notes of the nochturnal bird,
Of death premonished, some sick neighbour's knell.
I, too, remember once at midnight dark
How these sky-yelpers startled me, and stirred
My fancy so, I could have then averred
A mimic pack of beagles low did bark
Nor wondered I that rustic fear should trace
A spectral huntsman doomed to that long moonless chase.

Poet and newspaper
editor John Holland
(1794-1872)
Sheffield Libraries

AN OMEN OF DEATH

An instance of the power of super-stition on the minds of individuals, even in the present day, came before the notice of a Coroner's Jury, at Sheffield, on Monday last, at the inquest on the body of a child whose death had resulted from being accidentally choked with a piece of apple. One of the witnesses present at the child's death was a Mrs Smith, a woman advanced in years, but whose conduct shewed her to be of an affection-ate and sympathising disposition. Though the cause of death was clearly shewn to have been accidental, she could not be brought to agree in this opinion, but with many hums and ahs, expressed her doubts upon the matter, and on being pressed for what she thought had been the cause of death she at last, with some reluctance, expressed her belief that the child had been 'struck'. She then remarked, that on getting out of bed in the morning, she was forcibly impressed with the appear-ance of a strong light in the east, from which omen she knew that someone near her would be visited by death. Observing the incredulous smile with which it was received by the Coroner and the Jury, she shook her head very knowingly, and, as if in contempt of their ignorance, added: 'Ah, every body does not know what I know'. On being pressed to enlighten the Jury she said, that she had always believed the appearance of this remark-able strong light in the east was an omen of death, and she only remembered hav-ing seen it once before in her life, and on that very day her niece died.

Sheffield & Rotherham Independent, 13 November 1847

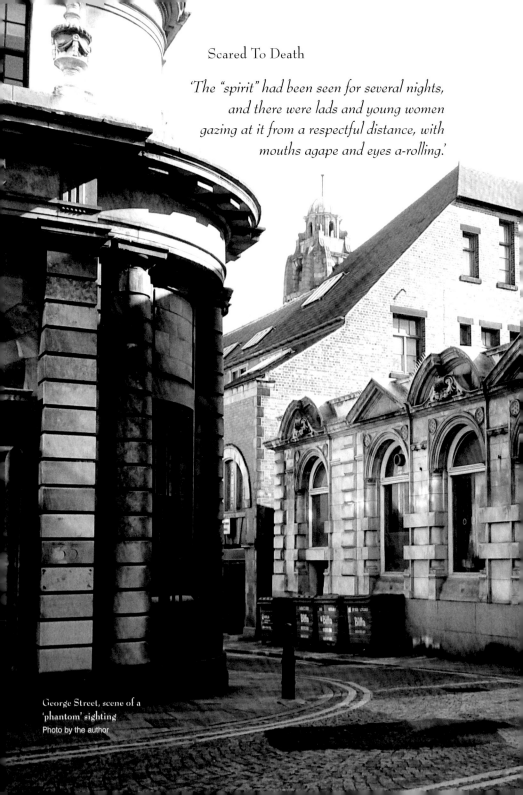

Scared To Death

'The "spirit" had been seen for several nights, and there were lads and young women gazing at it from a respectful distance, with mouths agape and eyes a-rolling.'

George Street, scene of a 'phantom' sighting
Photo by the author

4
PHANTOMS BY GASLIGHT

Before the early years of the 19th century Sheffielders were entirely reliant upon the fitful illumination provided by oil lamps and candles after nightfall. The first gas lamps arrived in the town centre in 1819 with the creation of the Sheffield Gaslight Company. Electric lights began to appear from the 1880s but public lighting did not arrive until 1907. Outside the town centre many of today's suburbs were simply hamlets or collections of cottages. At night the only lights visible would be flickering candle-lights in the windows of dwellings.

Innovations such as gas-lights and magic lanterns introduced new types of illumination to the streets of Victorian England that, in some cases, helped to create ghost experiences and panics. In 1801 Paul de Philipstahl took his Phantasmagoria ghost show to London and by 1820 the invention of limelight allowed magicians to produce a powerful illumination that could be directed and focused. The Scottish scientist David Brewster's *Letters on Natural Magic*, published in 1832, exposed magician's tricks with magic lanterns and sought to explain a variety of religious and supernatural visions as 'nothing but projected delusion' . Brewster's writings were widely read and may have provided inspiration for a story in Charles Dickens' *The Pickwick Papers*. A church sexton, Gabriel Grub, has his conscience pricked by a vision of 'officious goblins with a perpetual smile on their faces' whilst walking through a dark graveyard. The description of Grub's experience led one authority to suggest it was 'reminiscent of a magic lantern twin dissolve unit in operation'.

The most familiar show featuring projections of ghosts was that invented in 1863 by an engineer from Liverpool, Professor Pepper. 'Peppers Ghost' was a 3D illusion featuring an actor concealed in a pit below the stage whose image was projected onto a sheet of glass. The show became a box-office hit when it toured English towns and a version was exhibited at the Music Hall in Surrey Street, Sheffield, in 1867. An account published in *The Sheffield Telegraph* said visitors were astonished by 'ghosts...produced upon the stage, and made to perform some peculiar antics'.

There were many examples of optical illusions created in Sheffield's streets by the arrival of gaslights and other types of new-fangled illuminations.

PRELIMINARY NOTICE.

MUSIC HALL, SURREY-STREET.

FOR A SHORT SEASON ONLY,
COMMENCING TUESDAY, DECEMBER 26th, 1876
(Day after Christmas Day).

THE ORIGINAL PEPPER'S GHOST AND SPECTRAL OPERA COMPANY.

CHARLES DICKENS' CHRISTMAS CAROL.

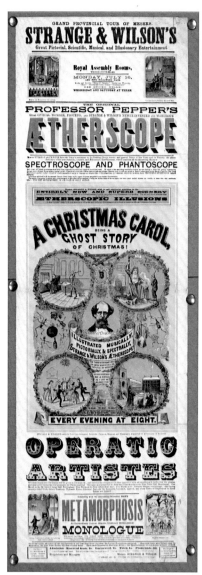

Poster for a Ghost Story show
British Library Board

Possibly the best known was the 'George Street ghost', mentioned in Henry Tatton's notes (see page 8). Tatton said this ghost 'operated where the side entrance to the Victoria Hall now is [off Chapel Walk]. At that time it was a wine and spirit merchants, and every night at a certain hour a white apparition appeared in the doorway. It was in the narrow part of George Street, just where the bend is, and people went and stood in awe to see the spirit appear'.

The mystery was investigated by a reporter from *The Sheffield Telegraph* who could not resist referring to 'Glenlivet, Old Tom and others of that ilk' in his story, published on 19 October 1882:

'One evening recently, passing through George Street, a congregation attracted my attention opposite the wooden gates of Messrs. Thomas Favell and Co., wine and spirit merchants."That's it!", "Isn't it plain?" "Oh!" &c,. &c. The "it," on inquiry, turned out to be "a spirit" which threw a white shadow on a door. Sure enough there was a shadow, which a lively imagination could easily fashion into the similitude of something ghostly in flowing garments. The "spirit" had been seen for several nights, and there were lads and young women gazing at it from a respectful distance, with mouths agape and eyes a-rolling'.

This apparition did not require an exorcist, as the intrepid reporter went on to explain: 'How soon the George Street ghost might have become a sensation is not known, for one of the onlookers, with no soul for the supernatural, put up his umbrella to shut off the reflection from the Norfolk Street lamp and presto! The ghost was gone!'

Henry Tatton wrote that: 'After investigation [the George Street ghost] was found to be caused by a reflection from a gas lamp just around the bend, which threw a light on a figure on the doorway'.

But the Norfolk Street gaslamp could not explain the phantom that puzzled passers-by in Barker's Pool during September 1875. A report in the *The Sheffield Telegraph* told how one dark evening the thoroughfare 'opposite the premises of Messrs Davies and Hubbard, was almost impassable with people whose eyes were upward, but not heavenward, turned. They were gazing intently at the upper windows of the building, where "a white figure" was discerned perambulating uneasily about from side to side, but particularly patronizing the central window. The crowd soon came to a conclusion. It was a ghost! To have a basis for a respectable ghost it is necessary to prove a previous "tragedy". Where the wish is father to the thought this is not a difficult process. It immediately occurred to several of the people that an apprentice boy had lost his life there in a mysterious manner, and of course this was his ghost walking about the upper chamber'.

The journalist mingled with the crowd and asked someone what they were gazing at. He was invited to look at the upper window and 'saw a light which looked to be moving about' but the pragmatic pressman refused to believe it was a ghost. Cue the appearance in the crowd of a police officer known as Charley. *The Telegraph's* account of what happened next follows:

'Charley appeared to have a considerable experience of ghosts, and his experience had made him skeptical of the white sheets, the spring-heeled boots and the awful phosphorus. Charley looked at the window, and then he looked to a lamp on the opposite side of the street. The sound of a window flapping with the wind fell on his ear. He laughed at the idea of there being any ghost, and, being an official responsible for his opinions, he refused to accept the notion of a fire, and started the unsentimental, but original and sensible suggestion that there was neither ghost nor fire – that "the white figure" was a light, that the light came from a lamp directly opposite, and that the motion of the light was due to the window flapping in the wind.

'A few minutes later a couple of figures appeared at the windows. These were not white, but black. They had no ghastly scrolls in their hands, but hammers, with which they fastened the restless wood. One of the pair put his head out of the window, assured the people, "it was all right," and the multitude – which at one time must have numbered over a thousand – seeing that "the ghost" was laid, walked away, and left the spirit of the apprentice – if apprentice there was – in peace!'.

"GHOST SHOWS" AND THE LAW.

A case was heard at the Shire Hall, Nottingham, on Saturday, in which the proprietor of a ghost show, at Stapleford, was prosecuted, and singularly enough the prosecutor was a police-sergeant named Pepper. The charge was one of performing a stage play without a license, and also of using a building which was not licensed for that purpose.—Mr. H. B. Clayton defended, and questioned the witnesses as to whether they saw real personages on the stage or only shadows. He said such classic dramas as "Hamlet" and "The Silver King" were played by means of the phantoscope, and appealing to the police-sergeant, asked if he had never heard of "Pepper's Ghost." The officer said that he had, but had never seen it; it was not his ghost. (Laughter.)—Defendant, Arthur Scottorn, stated that he had carried on his show in a large number of towns in Staffordshire, Derbyshire, Nottinghamshire, and elsewhere, and had never been asked about a license. He did not consider that he required a license, as his performance was that of a phantoscope.—The Bench fined Scottorn 50s., and three other defendants, who had taken part in the perform-ance, were ... 5s.

THE 'HEELEY GHOST' SCANDAL
or 'much ado about nothing'

One night in October 1870 members of the Heeley Burgesses' Association met in the Red Lion Inn to discuss what should be done to 'abate the nuisance and outrage that have been offered to the neighbourhood for many weeks past' by the appearance of a ghostly 'Woman in White' at midnight. During the meeting Councillor Hawksley revealed he had caught a local teenager dressed in women's clothing masquerading as the 'ghost'. The burgesses decided to issue a summons demanding a public apology from the boy or his parents.

In the meantime, the boy's father, a Mr Maxey, wrote to the *The Sheffield Telegraph*. In the letter he confessed that his son Frederick, age 15, had 'on Saturday evening last dressed himself in white for a short time, in boyish fun' having heard rumours about the ghost in the street. Maxey senior complained that his good name and that of his family 'should be talked about opprobriously in a public house... at a meeting supposed to be convened to put a stop to the so-called scandal'.

On 1 November *The Sheffield & Rotherham Independent,* published an account of proceedings at Sheffield Town Hall under the title 'The Heeley Ghost in Court' :

The Red Lion, Heeley
Sheffield Libraries

...the defendant was in the streets dressed in women's clothes and he frightened several children

THE "HEELEY GHOST" IN COURT

At the Sheffield Town Hall yesterday, before T.W. Rodgers, Esq., and T. Jessop, Esq., a lad named Frederick Maxey, residing with his parents at Heeley, was summoned on the information of Mr Councillor Hawksley, that 'he, on the 15th October ...did unlawfully go about the public streets and highways there situate, dressed in women's clothes, and was guilty of scandalous conduct, whereby Her Majesty's subjects then and there residing, passing and repassing, were alarmed and annoyed, and decency was openly outraged and the public peace disturbed, against the peace of our lady the Queen'.

The court was crowded with people from the neighbourhood of Heeley.

Mr Clegg appeared in support of the summons, and Mr Binney for the defence. Mr Clegg said that for some time past the people of Heeley had been very much annoyed by their children being frightened in the streets by a ghost and the following exchange took place:

'On the Saturday night... the defendant was in the streets dressed in women's clothes, and he frightened several children. All that the complainant required was that he should express regret for having so acted, and promise not to offend again. It was of the greatest importance that such a state of things should be stopped, as if children were frightened when young they never recover from it...

Mr Jessop: What age is the lad?

Mr Binney: He is 15 years of age.

Mr Rodgers remarked that the Bench did not think so much about the defendant's having frightened children as of his having offended against public decency. The law would reach such an offence and the Bench would certainly put it in force.

On looking at the defendant, however, he could not but think that he had been guilty merely of a frolicsome mischievous act for which he deserved punishment from his father or a severe reprimand. If it had been shown that a grown-up person had been going about the streets in women's clothes offending against public decency and those proprieties of life which ought to exist toward the opposite sex, he would take uncommon good care that he should have some difficulty in escaping a month's imprisonment at Wakefield...

Mr Jessop said it was a very foolish boy's trick and if it was not for his years he would be dealt with very severely.

The defendant then made the following apology: 'I am very sorry that I went out in women's clothes on the Saturday night referred to, and I will not do it again'.

The defendant's father said he would have made a similar apology at any moment. The summons was then withdrawn and the interested parties left the court.

Sheffield & Rotherham Independent, 1 November 1870

EXORCISING THE HERMITAGE STREET GHOST

Bones in an old wooden box

In April 1887 *The Sheffield Telegraph* reported a ghostly manifestation on Hermitage Street, off London Road, as follows: 'For some time there have been stories that at the house occupied by a worthy pot-hawker named Samuel Hague, and his wife, have been heard strange sounds – at unseasonable times – chiefly, of course in the witching hour of night. A dress maker, working late, was startled by heavy clanking as if a big man in stout boots was patrolling overhead. She threw away her needle and worked no more that evening'. Even worse, Mrs Hague had been startled on several occasions 'by screams as of a child in distress'.

Rumour had it that 'some time in the remote past a little child was "done for" and that the heavy boots heard by the seamstress were worn by the ruffian who did the deed. The child is supposed to be still about the premises, and when screams are heard he or she is trying to get away from [the] murderer, who is doomed to revisit... and will never leave off re-enacting his crime'. The old adage that 'Murder will Out' continued to preoccupy the gossips of the neighbourhood despite the fact that the oldest resident of the area could not recall any tragedy of the type imagined.

The sensation grew when Mr Hague discovered the remains of an old wooden box whilst leveling part of his backyard. The box contained bones and hair and soon the word on the street was that the secret of the haunted house was out. Police were called in to examine the contents of the box and 'true to their matter-of-fact method of looking at mysteries' they concluded they most likely belonged to a dog or fowl. The box was returned to Mr Hague and the officers advised him that it would make good firewood.

The Telegraph report ended: 'This suggestion has been acted upon and, last evening, Mr and Mrs Hague, leaving their dwelling to be surveyed – from the outside – by such as might feel disposed that way, betook themselves, like sensible people, to worship at their usual tabernacle, the "Happy House". Now, it is anticipated, the child-like screaming will cease to be heard, and the heavy boots potter about overhead no more'.

THE PROSAIC SIDE OF A "HAUNTED HOUSE."

Ecclesall, a division of Sheffield, in the region lying between Cemetery-road and Bramall-lane, is rich in haunted houses and dwellings endowed with mysterious and fearsome noises. The most notorious of recent manifestations was at Pearl-street, where crowds blocked the streets in the hope of hearing unearthly knockings coming from nobody knew where—until prosaic Inspector Bradbury, who will not allow even ghosts the poor privilege of obstructing a common-place thoroughfare, took it into his head to mount guard at a certain house, where he discovered the knocking was done by a meek-faced female of tender years, supposed to be too weak to clang anything against a wall. Now Hermitage-street—or, strictly speaking, Cross George-street—puts in a plea for attention. For some time there have been stories that at the house occupied by a worthy pot-hawker, named Samuel Hague, and his wife, have been heard strange sounds—chiefly, of course, in the witching hour of night. A dressmaker, working late, was startled by heavy clanking as if a big man in stout boots was patrolling overhead. She threw away her

5
SPRING-HEELED JACK

"If he wasn't the Devil, then who the devil was he?" Philip Pullman

One of the earliest mentions of the bogeyman that would inspire fear and anxiety in the minds of thousands was in February 1838 when the monster was named by *The Times* as the mysterious bugbear responsible for a series of assaults, mainly upon young girls, in the Barnes Common area of north London. Newspapers suggested this terror campaign began during the previous year in villages that formed the northern fringe of the growing metropolis.

Cover of children's book by Philip Pullman

Descriptions of Jack's appearance varied in the telling. Sometimes he appeared in animal form as a bull or bear, at others he wore a suit of armour. He had eyes of flame and employed metal claws or talons to rip at the clothes of his victims, but his most obvious characteristic was his ability to escape through tremendous leaps and bounds, popularly attributed to springs concealed in his boots.

Spring-heeled Jack was often portrayed as a demonic visitor. Among the wide diversity of early descriptions is one published by the *Morning Chronicle* in 1838 that refers to a figure clad in a bear's skin '...which upon being drawn aside, exhibited a human body in a suit of mail, and with a long horn, the emblem of the king of hell himself'. Later accounts refer to horns, sulphurous smells and blazing eyes. During the scare that gripped Sheffield in 1873, the wall of a cave from which the spring-heeled ghost emerged was painted with the words 'the Black Devil'.

Later in Victorian England Spring-heeled Jack became a generic street name for assorted criminals and footpads who leapt on their victims and made good their escape by speed and agility. In 1861 Henry Mayhew collected stories and legends from inmates of the capital's workhouses. One 16 year old boy told him the 'best men' in such tales were usually agile and cunning thieves who outwitted the police. These miscreants 'were always called Jack'.

The link with the criminal underworld also appears in *A Dictionary of English Folklore*, where Spring-heeled (or Springheel) Jack is defined as 'a general Victorian nickname for a street robber...and did not necessarily refer to one particular man'. Accounts of court proceedings from Victorian England often include examples of named individuals, 'known as a Spring-heeled Jack' in their localities, who were prosecuted for a variety of assaults, burglaries and anti-social behaviour.

'The exploits of Spring Heeled Jack are still remembered as having frightened London half out of its wits. The miscreant made night hideous by his tricks – leaping over hedges to the terror of lonely pedestrians, waylaying females, scaring children, and even rendering the drivers in charge of the mails helpless with terror. The suburbs of London were in a far different state forty years ago, when all this happened, to what they are now, and it can easily be imagined how great was the consternation thus occasioned among those residing in them. People were afraid to venture out after nightfall. Stories of the wildest and most extravagant nature got into the newspapers and formed the staple of conversation. For many Spring Heeled Jack was believed to be a veritable demon; others declared him to be a nobleman in disguise who took delight in his cruel sport; while the majority were in favour of his being a vulgar footpad, who first terrified those whom he subsequently plundered. Thus, while some credited him with horns and eyes of flame, an opposite set of eye-witnesses were in favour of a mask and whitened face; and society was divided between believers in hoofs, and those who asserted, with hardly less folly, that the extraordinary leaps in which he indulged were effected by means of springs in his boots, powerful enough, some said, to carry him over houses!'

News of the World, November 17, 1872

In 1869 a man called John Allott, 'alias Spring-heeled Jack', was fined by magistrates in Barnsley for poaching with a shotgun on land at Hemsworth. He fled when spotted by a gamekeeper but was not as swift-footed as his nick-name implied, as he was captured and hauled before the town's JPs.

Although the identity of the Spring-heeled Jack gang that terrorised London in 1837-38 was never proved beyond doubt, many writers have pointed an accusing finger at a nobleman, Lord Henry de la Poer Beresford, the 3rd Marquis of Waterford. Waterford and a small group of aristocratic friends were notorious for a series of cruel and vicious pranks that were chronicled in the newspapers of the day. These included practical joking that occasionally resulted in savage beatings of random pedestrians. As a symbol representing the excesses of the idle rich and the landed aristocracy, Waterford presented a convenient scapegoat for radical politicians and journalists, such as the editor of the London *Morning Post*, who published Spring-heeled Jack stories.

Marquis of Waterford

The involvement of 'some persons of the Waterford class' in Spring-heeled Jack's exploits was alleged in correspondence received by Sir John Cowan, the Lord Mayor of London, in January 1838. A 'resident of Peckham' who remained anonymous but may have been a woman, alleged that 'some individuals (of, as the writer believes, the higher ranks of life)' had laid a wager 'with a mysterious and foolhardy companion...to enter gentlemen's gardens for the purpose of alarming the inmates of the house'.

As a result of this wager, seven women had been 'deprived of their senses'. And as the story grew in the telling, so did the number of victims subject to the wager.

Another anonymous letter referred to the monster 'appearing in the guise of a ghost, bear, or devil, has been within the last week or two repeatedly seen at Lewisham and Blackheath. So much, indeed, has he frightened the inhabitants of those peaceful districts that women and children durst not stir out of their houses after dark'. Wilder versions spread to other districts of London, with tales of females being frightened to death and children torn to pieces'. Shortly afterwards another paper reported that 'the object of the villains is to destroy the lives of not less than thirty human beings'.

The anonymous letter sent to the Lord Mayor of London introduced the idea of a cover-up of Spring-heeled Jack's crimes by the aristocracy. The writer implied that the press had been 'induced to remain silent', presumably via the influence of the 'higher ranks' of the Waterford class. The idea of cover-ups by the police, the press and government also appear in the legends and rumours of the Jack the Ripper murders.The Marquis of Waterford was killed in a riding accident in 1859 and within a decade he was named by several sources, as the original perpetrator of the Spring-heeled Jack scare. Unfortunately for this theory, although there is some circumstantial evidence to place Waterford in London during the winter of 1837-38, there is no convincing evidence to support the allegation that he was responsible for all the assaults attributed to Spring-heeled Jack.

The earliest known depiction of Spring-Heeled Jack, 1838

Spring-heeled Jack also appeared both in dramatic theatrical productions and popular 'pulp' literature. The most prominent and influential example of the latter was the character portrayed in the Penny Dreadfuls, whose popularity reached its height in the mid-19th century.

As their name suggests, these publications were cheap illustrated serials containing lurid and sensational crime fiction. Spring-heeled Jack appears in Penny Dreadful serials between 1860 and 1904. Here he was portrayed not as a ghost or demon but as a vengeful anti-hero, often a wronged aristocrat, whose demonic appearance was complemented by spring-heeled boots, horns and bat-like wings.

Examples of Penny Dreadful covers depicting Spring-Heeled Jack
Author's collection

SHEFFIELD'S SPRING-HEELED JACK

Frightening figures and bogeymen are symbols of our fear of the unknown and the inexplicable. Within living memory they have been used by parents to tease and frighten misbehaved children. Bogeymen are an integral part of our childhoods and stories about them often form our first taste of adult life and the dangers that lie outside the safety of our homes.

Some bogeymen live on in the popular imagination, while others have been forgotten.

From an early age I heard stories from my grandparents about a character called Spring-heeled Jack whose name was uttered in fearful, whispered tones, almost as if speaking it aloud might be enough to summon it back to this world.

The warning 'behave yourself or Spring Heeled Jack will come for you' was frequently heard in their childhood as a means to strike terror into youngsters.

And, half a century later, I felt that same fear and dread.

For a child immersed in comic book superheroes, Spring-heeled Jack appeared to be a Victorian super villain who was waiting for a local Spider-man to bring him to justice.

My grandmother was emphatic that whatever he eventually became, Spring-heeled Jack was a real man of some description, 'a wrong'un from the Park' as she put it. When pressed for more details she told of a 'figure in white, wearing some sort of mask and cape' who had springs in his

Victorian cover of the story of 'Spring-Heeled Jack
Author's Collection

55

'It used to appear at all times of the night, robed in white, and suddenly appear in front of people, mostly courting couples, and then suddenly disappear when anyone tried to get hold of it.'

HENRY TATTON

boots' and appeared at night in lonely parts of the city, in Norfolk Park and around Heeley, where her family lived, leaping out on unsuspecting passers-by. Jack moved with uncanny speed and was able to leap over groups of people, fences and walls.

She understood that unlike Charlie Peace, whose natural agility and skill in disguising himself allowed him to evade capture, he was not directly guilty of any specific murder or robbery. Charlie Peace was a murderer but Spring-heeled Jack was a phantom who created real fear and anxiety. Fear that she, as a young girl, felt when walking alone at night in darkness, even though Jack's reign of terror in Sheffield ended before she was born.

The same fear and anxiety was recalled by Heeley resident Henry Tatton, who was just 12 years old when Spring-heeled Jack made his first appearance in the Park District during the spring of 1873.

Tatton's notebook refers to 'Spring-heeled Jack or the Park Ghost' as follows: '... it appeared at all times of the night and disappeared suddenly, before anyone could get hold of it. It mostly came out of the Cholera Monument Grounds. Springing and jumping about the quarry and over walls....crowds... went to see it and try to capture it'.

Tatton said when it 'got too hot' for the ghost, it moved its operations to other districts of the city. People were now afraid to go out at night and began to carry sticks to attack it. 'This went on for some time and the ghost had some very narrow escapes,' Tatton wrote. Eventually it ceased its marauding. Tatton added that it 'never came out who it was' but that 'it was said to be a member of a well-known family in the Park district who did it for sheer devilment'.

Gravestone at the Cholera
Monument Grounds

Depiction of Spring-Heeled Jack at Aldershot in 1877 Illustrated Police News

Another contemporary of the scare, writing in *The Sheffield Telegraph* in 1910, referred to a period in the city's history when 'epidemics of ghost alarms occurred', a favourite location being Clay Wood and the churchyard of St Mary's in Bramhall Lane.

At Clay Wood quarry, adjacent to the Cholera grounds, there was a haunted cave where, 'hundreds of people would congregate...at nights gazing expectantly at a yawning black hole underneath the Cholera Monument Grounds, the said hole being popularly supposed to communicate by way of an underground passage with the Manor Castle'. Mysterious tunnels such as the one supposedly linking the ruins of the medieval Manor Lodge with Sheffield Castle are mentioned frequently in the city's folklore. In the popular imagination, they often contained ghosts. The article noted that at this time 'these crowds talked of "Spring-Heeled Jack", who is even now shelved by the "Penny Horribles", but the ghost never walked'.

St Mary's, Bramall Lane, another haunt of Spring-Heeled Jack
Inset: Carved head on the church

A GHOST IN THE PARK

Sheffield's pressmen reported the appearances of Spring-Heeled Jack with a mixture of incredulity and outright disapproval. The weekly *Sheffield Times* was the most dismissive, chastising its rivals for 'pandering to that senseless sensationalism which feeds on ghost stories'. The city's two daily papers both published lengthy reports on 23 May 1873. *The Telegraph*, in a story headlined 'A Ghost in the Park', noted that a rumour had been in circulation since the Easter holidays before it received any notice outside the district. It explained how 'something in white' had begun making nightly appearances in the Cholera ground and the adjoining Clay Wood, formerly known as Spring Wood.

The tone of the account published by the rival *Sheffield & Rotherham Independent* is suggested by the subtitle, 'An Awful Story'. The paper attributed the scare to 'an inhabitant of those parts – probably venerable and of the credulous sex – [who], while returning home at the hour when churchyards yawn and graves give up their dead, was paralysed by the appearance of a most indisputable "ghost", arrayed in orthodox robes of white, and smelling, as a matter of course, of brimstone'.

The beholder promptly fainted and 'afterwards arrived at home with hair on end, and with such a tremendous story concerning hobgoblins and goblins, and apparitions and midnight specters, that the blood of all adjacent persons was curdled into an unnatural and unhealthy state'. Soon afterwards, other women and children complained about 'a tall man covered with a sheet' who sprang out in front of them in lonely places.

Cholera Monument Grounds

A GHOST IN THE PARK.
ATTACK ON THE POLICE.

During the last few days quite a sensation has been caused in the Park, and more particularly in the vicinity of the Cholera Monument, by the circulation of a report that "a ghost was to be seen!" The rumour first gained currency about a month ago, but like all ghost stories was discarded by sensible people. A few of the more curious, however, watched, but without success, although women and children complained of seeing "a tall man covered with a sheet" who met them in lonely places; occasionally, too, when the husband was out, women have been startled by the sudden entrance of the stranger into their dwellings. These complaints became numerous, and as the complainers had really been frightened, and serious results were likely to ensue in one or two cases, it was taken for granted that a ghost was appearing in the neighbourhood. The subject was well cultivated by newsmongers, and ultimately it was rumoured that a man, whose name has not been made public, wagered in Easter week to frighten a certain number of individuals between then and Whitsuntide. If he accomplishes his task and escapes the law, it is said he will receive a large sum for his trouble. Whoever the ghost may be, he selects his victims from the weaker sex, and rarely or never "appears" to any of the male inhabitants of the neighbourhood. Up to a fortnight ago his visits were confined to the districts of Bernard-street, Haigh-lane, and Cricket-road, but latterly he has appeared among the well-to-do people of Nor-folk-road, who have complained to the police of his operations. It is believed that he is assisted by others interested in his success, while another party is on the alert, and doing their utmost to catch and hand him over to the police. From eight to eleven o'clock last night Norfolk-road and the adjoining thoroughfares were filled with people from different parts of the town, and in their anxiety to behold the mysterious stranger. Others damaged the shrubberies of many of the residents. Others betook themselves to the quarry beneath the Cholera Monument, and as tokens of their presence made fires of old matting and other rubbish deposited there. It is ____ ___ __ say the ghost did not appear, but it

...a rumour spread that a 'ghost' was appearing nightly in the monumental gardens and nearby Clay Wood.

Stories told by women and children were not taken seriously, but the situation changed at the beginning of May when the 'ghost' began scaring the 'well to do' residents of the big houses on Norfolk Road, adjoining the Cholera grounds. They complained to the police. From that point onwards stories of the ghost's appearances spread rapidly and crowds gathered each night in the haunted district. *The Sheffield Telegraph* noted that 'it is believed that he [the ghost] is assisted by others interested in his success, while another party is on the alert, and doing their utmost to catch and hand him over to the police'.

Sheffield's newspapers called the apparition 'The Park Ghost'. Initially, no one mentioned 'Spring-heeled Jack' as the ghost would later become known, but *The Sheffield Times* referred to his 'spring-heels and phosphorus face, spitting fire', while the *Telegraph* referred to the ghost 'skimming over the ground with supernatural swiftness'. Similarly, a reporter from *The Sheffield Independent* described how the visitor 'refused in the plainest manner to have anything to say to anybody, and spent much of its time in scudding through the Cholera burial ground and steeple-chasing in a break neck away across the disused quarry'.

An illustration from The Illustrated Police News, December 1872 The British Library Board

Another reported how one eyewitness claimed that he saw the apparition clear a stone wall in one bound; the wall proving to be 14ft 3 inches in height. Another told how, after leaping upon two terrified young girls, he seized them and, after whirling them around, threw them over a stone fence. A third claimed a group of vigilantes had fired a shotgun at the ghost, but seemingly without any effect as he bounded away quicker than ever.

Nightly, crowds of ghost-hunters gathered in Norfolk Road and the Cholera grounds, armed with knives, guns and bulldogs. News of the scare reached as far as the London newspapers, who noted the role played by 'roughs' in the mayhem that followed.

On the night of Thursday, 22 May, according to a report in *The Sheffield Telegraph:* '...from eight to 11 o'clock Norfolk Road and the adjoining thorough-fare were filled with people from different parts of the town, and in their anxiety to behold the mysterious stranger damaged the shrubberies of many of the residents. Others betook themselves to the quarry beneath the Cholera Monument and as a token of their presence made fires of old matting and other rubbish deposited there. It is needless to say the ghost did not appear, but it was reported that he had been visiting very near'.

When attempts were made by police officers to disperse the mob they were pelted with sticks and missiles. For some hours mob law ruled. Two officers were severely injured as a result, including PC Ironside, who 'while at the top of South-street was struck on the head with a stone with such violence as to cause him to fall.' He was picked up by other officers who found he had suffered 'an ugly wound from which blood flowed freely'. The officer was carried to the Town Hall for treatment, 'and when the police disappeared, the crowd dispersed apparently of their own accord'.

On the following night, Friday 23 May, the situation worsened. Gangs of 'roughs', who were determined to lay the ghost, turned their frustration on the police.

A GHOST STORY.

TO THE EDITOR OF THE SHEFFIELD DAILY TELEGRAPH.

Sir.—I have a truthful ghost story to relate, and that person who can peruse this veracious chronicle and then deny the authenticity of supernatural phenomena deserves—well, I have not yet studied out the punishment he merits. To commence, a geographical sketch of the walk of my ghost is requisite. Ours is dubbed a terrace, which, thanks to the godfather who gave us our name, raises us in the estimation of our surrounding neighbours, who only live in "streets," or at the best unpretentious "roads." We, in the terrace, have each a spacious garden in the front of our domiciles, about ten feet by twelve, well adapted for the rearing of tall weeds and rank grass.

Now, on Sunday night the mistress of one of these abodes sat alone by her own fireside. The rest of the household were scattered far and wide. Suddenly a dull heavy thudding noise was heard against the window, which seemed to shake the house side. It was not a sharp crash, as though something had been thrown, but yet it seemed apparently sufficient to smash in the window, though no broken glass followed the concussion. A pet canary in a fancy cage, suspended in the centre of the window, dropped from its perch as though stricken dead by some invisible power. I am not prepared to vouch that the clock stopped, or that the fire burned blue, but if I carry out my vague, and at present undefined intention of proceeding on a lecturing tour on "Ghosts and Ghostesses," I shall go the whole hog and swear anything, and even probably manufacture cases to fit in; such proceedings being no doubt as honest as those of many of our Liberationist, C. D. Acts, and such like class of lecturers. But to resume: Again and again did the noise occur, accompanied by a peculiar scratching, or slight tearing of the glass.

Now, several years ago, our locality was visited by a celebrated ghost, who will be known to posterity as the Park ghost. What so natural, then, that the mistress of the house should deem this to be a return of that gentleman (for ghosts are as erratic as comets, and may return at any time), or at least one of his relations. But summoning courage she opened the door and looked out on the dreary

On this occasion 'not less than two thousand persons, principally youths and young men', according to *The Sheffield Independent,* 'congregated in the haunted district, much to the annoyance of the residents. A numerous staff of police officers was there ready to receive them. Shortly before ten o'clock a large crowd got together, and when the police attempted to disperse them they were attacked with stones. For several minutes showers of stones were hurled at the police, and several were struck on the body. A charge was then made, and a young man was captured, but after being detained by the police a short time, he was liberated. The crowd then began to disperse, and long before the traditional hour for the appearance of ghosts the district was almost entirely deserted.'

A report published by *The Telegraph* the following morning added some intriguing details about the hiding place of the 'ghost' that was being staked out by youths:

'Near the place where the apparition is once said to have disappeared is a large hole at the bottom of the quarry skirting the cholera burial grounds.

Many of a superstitious turn of mind were so credulous as to explore this miniature cave yesterday with candles, and it is said...that at the far extremity is painted on the face of the rock in large letters "the black devil"....Throughout the day special constables were on duty outside the cave entrance and towards dusk began to experience the greatest difficulty in keeping a clear passage along the thoroughfare.

'The day will long be remembered by many roughs whose apparent intention was to indulge in the similar kind of amusement to that which they enjoyed on the previous evening. The officers of justice were, however, too numerous for them to attack even in the cowardly way of stone-throwing. Having the forethought to provide themselves with canes the constables, whenever a justifiable chance was given, made vigorous use of them and by this means succeeded in keeping the rabble under control. The so-called spectre has not yet made another appearance'.

On Saturday, 24 May, a leader writer on *The Independent* appealed to the spectre: 'We beg of you...go to Hades or to the Red Sea – or anywhere, in short, out of Norfolk Road. A nightly battle between the police and the public on account of "something in white" cannot be gratifying to any well-organised supernatural being, and can only afford pleasure to a morbid evil minded spirit unfit for decent society'.

If the 'ghost' was a human prankster, as many believed, he was dissuaded from making further appearances in the Cholera grounds. Soon afterwards, reports of appearances elsewhere in the city began to spread.

GHOST HUNTING ON
THE STREETS OF SHEFFIELD

A journalist, who styled himself 'The Impartial Observer', joined a group of vigilantes hunting for the ghost in Pitsmoor. His account, published in *The Sheffield & Rotherham Independent*, on Saturday 31 May 1873 provides a neat insight into the atmosphere that prevailed among what leader writers described as 'the lower classes':

'Most of the would-be captors were armed with bludgeons of portentous thickness. Some half score or so had with them bull terriers of truculent aspect; one man had over his shoulder a double-barrelled gun, with a dose of No. 4 in each barrel, which he had benevolently prepared for the special benefit of his ghostship. Another amiable individual showed me a diabolical instrument, originally, I should think, a butcher's steel, but which he had carefully ground down to a tapering point as sharp as a needle; and with this improvised stilleto he coolly declared his intention of "letting light" into any unfortunate apparition with whom he might meet.

'There was one thing, however, in the ghost's favour - the "hunters" made noise enough to give ample notice of their approach; and, in addition, the ascending vapour from numberless pipes charged with the strongest (and vilest) of tobacco, diffused through the air far and wide an odour which any well-conducted apparition would instinctively fly.

'Loud and deep were the threats indulged in, for confident in numbers the most timid waxed valorous, and if the ghost had appeared he would, I fancy, have had a warm reception. No ghost was, however, encountered. A neighbouring church struck eleven, and what was of more consequence to the crowd, the neighbouring public house closed its doors. The watchers grew fewer and fewer - there was absolutely nothing to be seen - the man with the gun seated himself on the kerb stone, and

THE SHEFFIELD GHOST.—The excitement produced in the Park by the report that some supernatural being, attired in white, was to be seen there in the night-time, still continues, and is likely to do so for some time to come. Near the place where the apparition is once said to have disappeared is a large hole at the bottom of the quarry skirting the cholera burial grounds. Many of a superstitious turn of mind were so credulous as to explore this miniature cave yesterday with candles, and it is said, though we do not vouch for the accuracy of the statement, that at the far extremity is painted on the face of the rock in large letters "the black devil." Throughout the afternoon and evening special constables were on duty at the place, and towards dusk began to experience the greatest difficulty in keeping a clear passage along the thoroughfare. The day will long be remembered by "many roughs," whose apparent intention was to indulge in the similar kind of amusement to that which they enjoyed on the previous evening. The officers of justice were, however, too numerous for them to attack even in the cowardly way of stone throwing. Having the forethought to provide themselves with canes the constables, whenever a justifiable chance was given, made vigorous use of them, and by this means succeeded in keeping the rabble under control. The so called spectre has not yet made another appearance.

The Sheffield Telegraph, Saturday May 24, 1873

let loose a variety of expletives on ghosts in general and on this particular ghost especially. A cadaverous youth who, in company with a short pipe and a white bull dog, had been tramping backwards and forwards for some time, followed on the same side with great fervour and fluency. It was evident that "on this occasion", as play bills have it, the ghost declined to appear, and so giving it up as a bad job I and my friend strolled homeward, deeply disgusted with the lack of compliance on the part of the supernatural gentleman unknown whom we had come with the deliberate intention of interviewing'.

By the end of May 1873, ghost scares had been reported in Upperthorpe, Pitsmoor, Crookes and parts of the city centre. A number of these were the result of copycat pranksters. *The Independent,* for instance, reported on 26 May that 'something in white' had been spotted on Pitsmoor road near a quarry at the top of Nottingham Street.

'...not only was it seen, but it positively committed a cowardly little theft. How are the mighty fallen! A girl was returning from a public house with a jug of beer for her parents' supper, when his Ghostship made his appearance and behaved uncommonly like an inhabitant of this lower sphere, whose moral training was somewhat neglected – behaved in fact, to put it plainly, like a thief. He took the jug from the girl, drank the contents with an evident relish, and then vanished, not however into thin air, but over a wall'.

"....the man with the gun seated himself on the kerb stone, and let loose a variety of expletives on ghosts in general and on this particular ghost especially."

The ghost was seen prowling the streets of Upperthorpe, and 'flits to and fro with a meditative air, stroking a flowing beard, white with the snows of many sin-storms... it is said that this ancient spirit took a constitutional in Portland street the other night, and so terrified a girl that she was seized with a fit, and has since been confined to her bed'.

The ghost's activities had left the more superstitious inhabitants of the town in a state of anxiety: '...urchins go trembling to bed, and solitary pedestrians hurry through the streets, and start at every sound expecting, yet dreading, to see the spectre'.

On 31 May *The Telegraph* reported another appearance on Glossop Road, present-day West Street: 'A woman was passing up the causeway when she felt someone touch her on the shoulder, and on turning around saw "something in white" with large eyes. She fell senseless to the ground, and a man, who also witnessed "the apparition", ran off affrighted. The "ghost" was last seen making off in the direction of Gell-street. A crowd speedily collected and the woman was removed into an adjoining house, where she recovered sufficiently to be taken home'.

The level of commotion sometimes descended into farce. A court report published by *The Sheffield Telegraph* revealed how one Richard Rhodes, 'a middle aged man described as a cutler and banjo-player' was fined 20 shillings and jailed for one month for assaulting a police officer who he had mistaken for 'the ghost'. Sheffield magistrates heard how PC Turner was walking along Whitehouse Lane at Upperthorpe when Rhodes rushed at him in an excited state, exclaiming 'he would settle him'. The officer tried to calm him down but for his pains was struck violently over the head with Rhodes' banjo. 'The prisoner was then secured and conveyed to the police station,' the report continued, 'where he made a statement to the effect that he had mistaken the constable for "the ghost" and that as he "was not afraid of no ghoses" he rushed towards him.'

On 7 June *The Sheffield Times* announced confidently that 'the ghost has gone', his exit coinciding with the end of the Whitsun holidays. By this stage a number of theories were current in the city. What *The Independent* called 'strong minded persons' refused to believe a ghost existed at all and attributed the stories to 'the fervid imagination of divers old women and children.' Another group, 'although their number is very limited', believed that one of the occupants of a grave in the Cholera burial ground had lately become 'uneasy' and was compelled at certain seasons to leave his resting place.

The first book about Spring-Heeled Jack by Peter Haining, published in 1977

By far the most popular explanation was that the ghost was a local man who had taken a wager to appear as a ghost. *The Telegraph* noted a rumour current on 23 May that 'a man, whose name has not been made public, wagered at Easter week to frighten a number of individuals between then and Whitsuntide...if he accomplishes the task and escapes the law, it is said he will receive a large sum for his trouble'. *The Independent* reported the person in question was 'a young fellow of weak intellect, who has undertaken to appear nightly from Easter until Whitsuntide, for a wager of £50, which sum he is to forfeit if he fails to make his appearance nightly.'

The Sheffield Times upped the bet to '£100 [on the condition that he] is bound to appear in white at a number of principal localities... Broomhill and Broomhall are talked of as likely places for his next visit'.

THE BOGEYMAN RETURNS

The true identity of the man or men hiding behind the disguise of Spring-heeled Jack, or the reason for their activities, was never revealed. But stories and rumours about 'the ghost' refused to go away. Late in November 1873 a resident calling himself Observer wrote to a weekly newspaper, *The Rotherham and Masbrough Advertiser,* asking the editor: 'Can you enlighten the public as to there being any truth in the report that a man who goes by the name of "Spring-Heeled Jack" is frightening persons night after night in the vicinity of Rotherham?'. Observer's letter continued:

> **'Whether there exists such an individual or not, it is certainly necessary that some step should be taken to dispel the alarm which has been excited. It is not to be supposed that the police have been unable to meet with anyone who corresponds to the descriptions given of this mysterious man, for scarcely two of them are alike, and their number is legion; in fact I never heard or read of anyone assuming the various characters given of him, and performing such wonderful feats. Suffice my giving a few of the descriptions which have been narrated to me, in some cases the parties fully believing their story to be true – to a great extent – but admitting that they thought it somewhat exaggerated. First of all he is said to possess springs in his boots which enable him to jump over persons, walls, gates, hedges, with the greatest facility, can also tap at second-storey bedroom windows, climb up houses and disturb the inmates, by crying down the chimneys, all which things he is said to have done.'**

The account continued with further descriptions of Spring-heeled Jack's costume and exploits. According to the stories heard by Observer:

> **'...he wears a kind of white skull cap which is capable of being changed into a black cloud immediately he confronts any person.... He carries a lamp which can be converted into the imitation of a man's face, thus frightening people, and one woman actually thought that it was this wonderful lamp, which gave him power to jump over gas-lamps. Fourthly, he is reported to wear a coat of mail, which protects him from any ordinary blows which he might be subjected to....People are reported to have been made ill from the fright which he has given them, others having been robbed of wearing apparel.**
>
> **'He chiefly confines himself to attacking women, sometimes in a ghostly manner by suddenly making his appearance and then departing, at other times he assumes the more human form and condescends to touch them, and occasionally deprives them of some article of clothing as a memento, and even last night he has said to have had a desire for beer, and so took a jug filled with that beverage out of a child's hands; thereupon a man seized him, but he was found to be superhuman, and could not be held. Whether there be any truth in the story or not, great fear is excited.**

'Parties are going about with revolvers, and perhaps someone who is compelled to go out in the dusk, and bears any resemblance to the descriptions given, may meet with an unwelcome salute'.

Rumours of fresh appearances continued to reach the newspapers through the remainder of the decade. Spring-heeled Jack had become, by this time, a familiar character to most Victorians from his appearances in the Penny dreadfuls. Sheffielders were also familiar with a more harmless version who featured in the ghost shows that occupied a prominent place in the city's annual Christmas fair at Pond Hill. Show-people were always quick to adopt characters from popular folklore and from 1874, after the first Park ghost scare, the Christmas fair featured a 'hobgoblinscope' whose principle attraction was a character called 'Spring-heeled Jack of Rotherham'.

Meanwhile, during the autumn of 1875, *The Sheffield Telegraph* announced the return of the long winter nights had brought 'his ghostship of the Park' out of his hiding place. In August 'it was stated that he had been "seen" in the vicinity of that quarry he was so fond of jumping over in his wonderful spring-heeled boots'. But nothing further was heard from him until December 1887, when a writer on the same newspaper asked readers if 'Spring-heeled Jack had made his customary winter appearance' as 'about Broomhill and further afield there are strange stories about "the ghost"'. He continued:

'I have never met one yet who has seen "Jack" or his spring-heels, but there are scores of folks who know somebody else who met a man whose mother or sister or relative think they saw him. Fourteen years ago a friend accompanied me on a midnight perambulation around St George's Church, "in the witching hour of night". From information received "Jack" was to be in that neighbourhood. It was very cold, and the spring-heels did not appear. We waited an hour, and then went home to bed, feeling rather ashamed of our spring-heeled friend. But why Broomhill this season? What has the Park done amiss to be thus jilted? From time immemorial the Cholera grounds and the Duke's Quarry have been the legitimate home of Spring-heeled Jack. What is there at Broomhill to attract the spiritual? A really respectable ghost, with any pretensions to antiquity, would never leave the old Park for a brand-new place of glittering shops, cabs, and omnibuses like Broomhill. Everything seems to be degenerating now-a-days. Even ghosts are forsaking the good old ways in which their forebears walked'.

THE PARK GHOST AGAIN.

The rumoured reappearance of the Park Ghost caused a large number of persons to assemble last evening in Norfolk road and the neighbourhood, impressed with the laudable desire of catching the troubled spirit. Various rumours are current respecting the origin of the mystery. Certain strong-minded persons persist in stating that the Ghost only has an existence—so far as it is consistent with the character of a Ghost to exist—in the fervid imagination of divers old women and children. Others of a sporting turn of mind say that the Ghost is a young fellow of weak intellect, who has undertaken to appear nightly from Easter until Whitsuntide for a wager of £50, which sum he is to forfeit if he fails to make his appearance nightly. There are others again, although their number is very limited, who believe that one of the occupants of a grave in the Cholera Burial Ground has lately become "uneasy," and is compelled at certain seasons to leave his resting place. The sporting opinion receives the most credence, and hopes are expressed that in a few days the Ghost may be compelled to make a bodily appearance in the Police-court. On Thursday evening a large number of persons congregated in the vicinity of the Cholera Monument, and having fixed the quarry adjoining the burial ground as a rendezvous, lighted several fires in it. They then separated, and diligently sought for the nocturnal disturber of the public peace, but returned to the quarry without having made any discoveries. To keep the fires burning they pulled several trees to pieces before the police could interfere, and eventually commenced stoning the constables for want of a better occupation. Last evening not less than two thousand persons, principally youths and young men, congregated in the haunted district, much to the annoyance of the residents. A numerous staff of police-officers were there ready to receive them, and dispersed them as soon as a large number met

OUR LOCAL LEGEND

Spring-heeled Jack continues to stalk the collective memory of the people of Sheffield, 150 years after his appearance in the Park District. To paraphrase Peter Ackroyd's account of the original 'Terror of London', perhaps Sheffield's ghostly equivalent 'emerged from the streets themselves, like a golem which is supposed to be made from the mud and dust of a certain vicinity'.

When I first wrote an account of the legend for *The Sheffield Star* in 1987 few of the generation who remembered the bogeyman remained alive and Spring-heeled Jack was largely forgotten. But today he has re-emerged as an integral part of the city's supernatural folklore.

The number of internet references and imaginative interpretations of the legend, both in verse and drama, have increased every year. A 2003 thread on the Sheffield Forum discussion board produced numerous snippets of lore including stories about Jack 'jumping between the tower blocks' at Norfolk Park. These were built during the 1960s. Another contributor connected the legend with a burglar known as Spiderman, who used to climb walls to enter flats and offices during the 1980s.

In 2004 local historian Peter Machan cleverly used Spring-heeled Jack in a short story to mark the opening of the Norfolk Heritage Trail. The story is set on Fright Night the annual Hallowe'en festival in the city centre that attracts thousands of visitors dressed as ghosts, vampires and ghouls. Spring-heeled Jack is disturbed by the mayhem above ground and emerges from his hiding place in the caves beneath the monument. But his search for a suitable victim is thwarted by the unexpected intervention of the city's new-fangled Supertram.

Machan's story is illustrated with a photograph of a curious wooden carving that depicts a leaping bogeyman figure. The City Council's online guide to the Norfolk Heritage Trail says this can be found on the exterior of the city's oldest surviving domestic building, the Old Queen's Head public house, on Pond Street.

The caption reads: 'he [Spring-heeled Jack] is a legendary figure thought to live in tunnels below the city, who would jump out to scare people. He was able to jump great distances and reportedly leapt over high walls'.

Revellers at
Fright Night

The Old
Queen's Head,
Sheffield Libraries

The Old Queen's Head was made for the Talbot family in 1475 and was built in the traditional English style, from massive oak pillars.

In the earliest surviving records it is described as 'the hawle at the Poandes'. It may have been built as a lodge for Sheffield Castle but after the Civil War it appears to been used as a laundry for the Talbots at the Manor Lodge. The link with these two ancient buildings might have encouraged the idea that the three places were linked by a network of underground tunnels, now blocked up.

At one time the Old Queen's Head, which stood alone since at least 1736, contained much rich and beautiful carvings. Over the years it has undergone many changes of ownership and became a public house in 1851. Many interesting interior features have been lost as a result of the severe treatment the building received during the 19th century. One of the few original features to survive are a series of carved female heads that project like corbels from wooden exterior panels.

These date from at least the 15th century and the image identified so 'Spring-heeled Jack' actually predates the ghost scare of 1873 by three centuries. Its grotesque appearance has always attracted comment and speculation.

When in 1895 Sidney Addy asked residents of nearby houses what they knew about the carving, he was told it was called 'Jonah', after the Biblical character who was swallowed by a whale. Addy wrote: '[it] represents either a man or a woman coming out of a fish's mouth [and] is of ruder execution than the others'.

Top: The Turret House at Manor Lodge, said to be linked via tunnels to The Old Queen's Head

Right: Carvings from the Old Queen's Head. The one on the right has been described as Spring Heeled Jack

Photo by the author

THE CHOLERA MONUMENT

By the early 19th century, with the Industrial Revolution in full swing, the population of Sheffield expanded rapidly. As numbers were swelled by immigration from the countryside, the living conditions of those working in the steelworks, mines and cutlery industry deteriorated. By 1820, the slopes of Park Hill had become a warren of cottages, alleyways and back-to-back slums.

Thousands lived in squalor and insanitary conditions were a breeding ground for disease. The most dreaded of all was the Asiatic cholera, that arrived in England in 1832 and spread rapidly through the Sheffield slums, taking more than 400 lives. The disease was caught by drinking water contaminated by untreated sewage. It struck quickly, with some poor victims taken ill in the morning and dead by the evening.

In the Park district the disease was both virulent and fatal and bodies were buried quickly in a communal grave, transported 'four or five together in a cart without sides or covering'. A resident of Heeley, writing in 1888, said 'one of my earliest recollections is of the general dread and alarm of the inhabitants of the town at that time, and of seeing the pots of pitch or tar burning in the yards and alleys, and also of the death of a neighbour's child after a few hour's illness'.

Before the true cause of cholera was understood, it was regarded as a disease of 'the poor, the ill and the drunk'.

Cholera Monument, Norfolk Park
Photo by the author

The falsity of that belief is evident from the single individual gravestone in the cemetery, marking the final resting place of the serving Master Cutler, John Blake. Of 292 victims buried in the cholera grounds between August and October 1832, 62 came from the Park Hill district.

Today, the 70ft tall Cholera monument that towers over the city's Midland railway station, marks the main communal grave. The plot of land off Norfolk Road, adjoining Clay Wood, was donated by the 12th Duke of Norfolk in 1835. The original shaft was surmounted by a plain cross and inscribed on three sides with the emblems of faith, hope and charity. The foundation stone was laid by the poet James Montgomery in December 1834, two and half years after the first outbreak of the disease in Sheffield. The builder, on being told the monument was not straight, responded, 'that was its beauty; anyone could build a thing straight'.

By then elegant stone-built villas and large houses with stables had been built on Norfolk Road, starkly emphasising the social divisions between the well-to-do and working class residents of the Park. Nevertheless, memories of the horrors of cholera and fate of the victims lingered in the collective memory. Later in Queen Victoria's reign the Cholera burial grounds were described as 'a gloomy spot...selected by a discerning and appreciative ghost as a fit place for a nocturnal visitation'.

Other victims of the epidemic are buried in the parish churchyards at St Mary's, Bramhall Lane and St George's, at the corner of Portobello and Mappin Street. It is interesting that both graveyards became the focus of ghost alarms later in the Victorian period.

Twice in its history the Cholera monument has been severely damaged in storms, most recently in 1990 when only the base of the original structure was left intact. Soon afterwards, with support from the Heritage Lottery Fund, the monument and the ornamental grounds that surround it were restored. The work included the opening of a heritage walk linking key landmarks in Sheffield Park with the city centre, and the installation of interpretative features commissioned from a local artist, Roger

Stainless Steel panel by Roger Gibson

Gibson. He created new designs for the gates that were 'both contemporary and in keeping with the gothic monument' including 16 stainless steel panels illustrated with themes that reflected the past and present.

The left gate features the Norfolk crest, a skull, smoky factory chimneys, cholera bacteria and 'Spring-heeled Jack – a local ghost'.

FROM HELL
Spring Heeled Jack and The Ripper

Jack was a popular name among hell raisers, highwaymen, pirates and unruly squires and the name turns up frequently in nursery rhymes and fairy tales. Jack Frost, Jack-in-the-Green and Jack o'Lantern are sinister figures but the epithet is most notoriously associated with the serial killer known as 'Jack the Ripper' who murdered at least five women in the Whitechapel area of East London in 1888-89. This label was adopted widely after the Central News Agency received a letter bearing the signature in September 1888. Before the name stuck, the murderer had been known as 'Leather Apron', a nickname common amongst slaughterhouse-men.

Many other letters claiming to be from Jack were received by the press and the Metropolitan police in 1888-89. One was signed: 'Spring Heel Jack, The Whitechapel Murderer'. This attempt to forge a link between the two bogeymen never quite caught the popular mood, but the level of fear and anxiety the brutal murders generated across the country led the Ripper to adopt some of the legendary characteristics previously associated with Spring-heeled Jack in the popular imagination. Today, mention of the Ripper continues to invoke images of a demonic figure in a cloak and a top hat stalking misty Victorian alleyways in search of his victims. Persistent rumours associate him with an aristocratic conspiracy, much like his spring-heeled namesake. Thus a faceless murderer moved from the slums of the East End into urban folklore.

A leader writer in the *Sheffield Evening Telegraph* (15 November 1888) summarised the effect of Jack's crimes on the population of Victorian Sheffield.

Even though the city was hundreds of miles from the atrocities committed in London, he wrote that '...the inhuman ghoul of Whitechapel has seriously shaken the national nerve. Far and near is the terror of him spread. Glancing over the list of police court cases, one cannot help being struck by the popularity which the title "Jack the Ripper" enjoys among the criminal classes. Simple in sound and vividly suggestive in meaning, the name has at once appealed to the excited imaginations of the mob...

'The public like nicknames for those about whom they are daily thinking and speaking and "Jack the Ripper" has entered the national mind as did the dreadful dragons of classic times, or the even more horrible devils, goblins and vampires of more recent days. Every drunken man in the country either imagines that he himself or somebody whom he sees is the identical assassin after whom the wildest hue and cry of the century is abroad'.

And he warned: 'Should the craze be allowed to go much further, and "Jack the Ripper" continue his unhallowed work with impunity, we may yet find ourselves plunged backwards into the abyss of popular superstition. Two hundred – or even one hundred – years ago the impenetrable mystery which surrounds the atrocious murders of Whitechapel would inevitably have led to the ignorant belief that they had been committed by no human hand. We have been educated beyond that now-a-days, but it rests with ourselves to see that we do not slip back again'.

A page from The Illustrated Police News in 1876, showing various types of ghosts and apparitions

6
SPIRIT-
RAPPINGS

Modern spiritualism was founded in 1848 following an outbreak of 'spirit rapping' in a farmhouse at Hydesville in New York State. The farm was home to the Fox family whose daughters Katie, 12, and Margaret, 15, claimed to have established communication with a poltergeist ('noisy ghost') by commanding it to copy the sound of their hand claps. Neighbours were understandably alarmed and some suggested the sounds were caused 'by a spirit of the dead or the devil himself'.

New York state was at that time a breeding ground for new religious sects and news of the mysterious rappings spread quickly around the world. The first message had been sent by electric telegraph four years earlier and spiritualism arrived just at the right time to take full advantage of great scientific, religious and social changes. In North America and Eu- *from the dead hour of Night, when all Things are buried in Sleep and Darkness, till the Time of Cock-crowing.'* rope, the Hydesville story triggered a wave of experimentation in Victorian homes. Although on the surface it appeared to be a typical case of a 'haunted house', what made this outbreak different from others was the idea that gifted human mediums could communicate directly with the spirits of loved ones.

Before the arrival of spiritualism there were a range of folk beliefs about the nature and purpose of ghosts. Most important of these was the idea that those who had died a tragic or bad death could appear to deliver a message, expose a crime or lead someone to hidden treasure. But many 'ghosts' were purposeless spirits that roamed the world 'from the dead hour of Night, when all Things are buried in Sleep and Darkness, till the Time of Cock-crowing'.

After the Reformation, during the Elizabethan period in England, ghostly manifestations tended to be blamed upon the devil or the results of witchcraft. For the elite, distinguishing between ghosts and demons remained a serious problem. The Presbyterian minister John Flavell (1630-91), for instance, accepted that God might sometimes send back the souls of the dead 'to evidence against the Atheism of men', but more often he believed ghosts were evil angels sent by the devil to mislead them.

By the 19th century doubt had been cast upon the teachings of the Bible and, even before publication of Charles Darwin's *The Origin of Species* in 1859, new discoveries and ideas such as evolution were leading many educated people towards religious skepticism.

Spiritualism appealed to all social classes and appeared to offer a bridge between agnosticism and the Christian faith. With death a frequent visitor to the Victorian household, and a high infant mortality rate, many people were willing to embrace aspects of spiritualism as it offered – unlike the church - empirical 'proof of immortality and the joy of renewed contact with lost loved ones'.

Celebrity endorsement added to appeal of spiritualism. Queen Victoria herself was said to have consulted mediums after the death of her beloved Prince Albert. Gladstone, Tennyson, Dickens and many others became fascinated with unexplained phenomena and the supernatural. Some of the leading scientific minds of the Victorian age, including the chemist Sir William Crookes, the physicist Sir Oliver Lodge and the radio pioneer Gugleilmo Marconi became convinced that communication with the spirits of the departed was possible.

In America, Thomas Alva Edison, the inventor of the phonograph and camera, was obsessed with creating a device that would allow him to talk to the spirit world. The logic employed by all these pioneers was simple: if people could communicate across the world via a telegraph cable, why couldn't the living communicate with the dead?

Spiritualism spread to Britain and quickly took root in the crowded industrial towns and cities in northern England. In 1852 an American woman, Mrs Hayden, began advertising her services as a spiritualist medium in England. *The Yorkshire Spiritual Telegraph*, founded in Bradford, Yorkshire, in 1853, was set up to record 'extraordinary communications from the spirit world', and before long spiritualist circles were established in many towns and cities.

At first these small gatherings consisted of friends and neighbours, with sittings providing a safe environment for young mediums to harness and practise their skills. In the early days of spiritualism the most common methods used by mediums developed out of parlour games that were popular during the 1850s. These included hat turning, table-tipping and spirit rapping. Typically, a group of seven or eight people would sit around a table in a darkened room, their hands lightly touching. An elected spokesperson would then address questions directly to the spirits, who responded via a system of raps, signalling 'yes' or 'no'. As the religion developed and mediums became more skilful, more elaborate devices appeared to improve communication with the spirits, such as printed alphabets and Ouija boards.

AMONGST THE SHEFFIELD SPIRITUALISTS.

RAISING A GHOST.

(By our own Medium.)

I have seen a ghost—at least, so I have been told—and he was certainly in a very good state of preservation. I have long been anxious to see "one raised from the dead," and have a very distinct recollection of having waited hours in a most unenviable position in the Park in the hope of obtaining a glance at the restless but mercenary spirit which perturbed the minds of peaceable inhabitants of that district about two years ago. On that occasion disappointment was my only reward, but now, through the instrumentality of Mr. E. Bullock, of London, the scales have been removed from my eyes, and I have seen the materialised spirit of Mr. Daniel Watt. This gentleman, who, it is perhaps unnecessary to remark, is defunct, was wont to reside at Camberwell, but whether he bore any relationship to the engineer who rendered that name distinguished, or

Some skilled mediums produced automatic writing during their trances and the spirits they claimed to have contracted were invited to play musical instruments, levitate people or furniture and, on occasions, even materialise in visible form.

Although the leading male medium of the period was Daniel Dunglas Home, many were women. Alex Owen in his book *Women, Power and Spiritualism in 19th century England*, said spiritualism offered women a respectable means of 'access to the public world' in Victorian society.

One of the most famous physical mediums of the period, Florence Cook (born 1874), was a working class girl from Hackney. From the age of 14 she began to experience spontaneous, trance-like states and 'flashes of clairvoyance, visions, noises in the head' and other spirit manifestations. She soon found herself a frequent houseguest of the wealthy and powerful and her activities brought her 'attention, status and material reward' that would never have been available to a girl from her social background.

Charles Dickens was fascinated by spiritualism and mesmerism and through them developed an interest in the power of the human mind. Unlike others who embraced the new religion, he refused to accept the existence of spirits until he was provided with some evidence. A number of mediums were exposed as frauds and charlatans, and in 1888 Margaret Fox – one of the sisters credited with the creation of the religion – publicly confessed the whole story was a hoax. To the horror of the spiritualists, she demonstrated to a public gathering how the sisters had produced the 'spirit rappings' by cracking her toe joints on a small pine platform.

Skepticism was growing even amongst members of the Society for Psychical Research, founded in Cambridge in 1882 to investigation alleged supernatural phenomena. Despite the publication of disparaging reports on the fraudulent activities of some well-known mediums, many sincere spiritualists remained convinced they had witnessed extraordinary phenomena – including contact with deceased loved ones - that could not be explained by science.

In Sheffield and other parts of the industrial north, groups of spiritualists began to organise séances and invited celebrity mediums to demonstrate their skills. In August 1876 a skeptical journalist from *The Sheffield and Rotherham Independent* joined a public séance held in Wells' dining rooms on Pinstone Street.

The reporter was keen to see a ghost as he had a 'very distinct recollection of having waited hours in a most unenviable position in the Park in the hope of obtaining a glance at the restless but mercenary spirit that perturbed the minds of peaceable inhabitants of that district' two years earlier.

The cynical newspaper-man emerged into the daylight disappointed, despite having witnessed table-turning, instruments floating in the air and a disembodied hand that was felt by several persons in the séance-room.

He returned the next day for 'private sitting' during which the medium, a 'Mr E. Bullock from London', was strapped into a chair behind a screen. 'Scarcely two minutes had elapsed before a hand, suspiciously resembling that of the medium, was thrust through an aperture in the screen,' he reported. 'An enthusiastic spiritualist promptly exclaimed "Thank you" and Mrs Bullock, the mother of the medium, expressed with considerable fervour her gratification that "Lillie had come back again once more" and hoped that she would do what she could for the friends present'. 'Lillie' proceeded to play a guitar, rang a bell and pushed a fan through the screen. All these items, the journalist pointed out, had been placed behind the screen before the séance began.

The sitters then attempted to put questions to the 'spirit' who was encouraged to write a message in a book placed on the medium's knee. After a few minutes the book was produced with the letters 'L W' (Lillie White) stencilled in large Roman capitals on the front page. On release from the chair Mr Bullock 'appeared to be asleep' or in a trance and 'to all appearance the straps...had not been tampered with, but, as everyone knows, appearances are deceptive'.

Afterwards the journalist wrote that despite having witnessed 'manifestations' he remained 'firmly convinced that there is nothing whatever in spiritualism and that, like most other American "inventions" it was brought into existence from interested motives'. That Mr Bullock was clever he did not deny, 'but I do deny that he has done anything that has not been done by professors' – the Houdinis and Derren Browns of the Victorian age - who claimed to be able to reproduce all the manifestations reported without calling upon the spirit world.

THE GHOST AT STORRS HALL

Outside the séance room, epidemics of 'spirit rapping' were reported across the nation. Even tiny rural communities experienced these panics.

In 1878 *The Illustrated Police News* published a story describing 'the doings of a supposed ghost' that had 'caused considerable alarm amongst the good people of Storrs, a hamlet on the borders of the Yorkshire and Derbyshire moors'.

Despite its title the newspaper, founded in 1863, had no connection with the police force but it was the first truly successful British publication to tap into the public's desire for news of crime, scandal and the macabre.

Voted as the 'worst newspaper in England' by a poll in 1886, it sold up to 200,000 copies in the big cities. The IPN contained just three pages of text, but the graphic and often lewd illustrations that adorned the front page outraged and fascinated prudish Victorians in equal measure. In the edition dated 19 January 1878 Storrs Hall was described as 'a romantic place' at Stannington, near Sheffield, with a history of hauntings by unaccountable noises, 'but by some means the ghost was laid, and until Christmas week [1877] nothing more was heard about it'.

By that time time the farm was owned by a Mr J. Wragg but the hall was occupied by James Ibbotson, his wife, her sister and a 14-year-old servant girl.

According to the *Police News*, 'mysterious rappings were heard, doors were thrown open, windows were broken, and strange noises were heard. Servants, armed with hayforks and anything that came in handy, issued forth immediately the knocks were heard, but they never discovered anything, and on no occasion did the ghost condescend to show itself'.

The story was covered in more detail by *The Sheffield & Rotherham Independent* on 5 January 1878. It reported how, during Christmas week, 'when the farming man and his maid were milking, persons came running out of the house greatly alarmed. Someone, they said, had been rapping at the door; but when the door was opened, no one could be seen. The man went into the house and stationed himself behind the door and the rapping was repeated, but still no one could be seen or heard. Subsequently, windows were broken both in front and at the back of the house. Watch has been kept both outside and inside, but the offender has not been discovered'.

By this point Mrs Ibbotson was so scared of the ghostly noises that she threatened to quit the house unless it was guarded by a policeman. *The Independent* reported that '...it is somewhat remarkable that a glazier was sent to repair the broken windows. He had no sooner repaired the window in front then it was again broken'. On this occasion the owner, Mr Wragg, was present in the house, along with Mr Ibbotson, her sister and a police officer, but they failed to discover how it was done. Wragg offered ten shillings to anyone who could solve the mystery and *The Independent* noted how, 'during the weekend the hall was visited by hundreds of

Storrs Hall, Stannington Photo by the author

people from Sheffield and the district around [and]...a number of men armed with stout sticks were watching outside the house but they failed to detect the offender. The fields around the hall were perambulated but no answers were found'.

Behind the sturdy walls of the hall, Police Sergeant Hobson, who had travelled to Storrs from Hillsborough police station, had already laid the ghost. 'Having carefully examined outside the premises, he was satisfied that the windows had not been broken by throwing at them from the outside,' the newspaper reported.

'He then proceeded to examine inside the house and, from what he saw, he was led to suspect the servant girl. He questioned her and she at first denied having any knowledge of the mischief. She then admitted she had broken one square with a can. Being further questioned she at last, after being much pressed, admitted that she was the real "ghost" and had broken all the windows with stones and done all the rapping; she had also cut the clothes line and thrown the clothes into the road.

'When the farming man was watching behind the door she stepped out of the cow-house where she was milking, and rapped at the door undiscovered. So coolly and warily had she affected the mischief that even her mistress did not suspect her when Sergeant Hobson began his interrogations'.

The paper added: 'The girl's name is Ann Charlesworth, aged 14 years, and her parents reside at Carr Head, near Deepcar. She cried bitterly after she had confessed and promised she would not repeat the offence'.

THE PEARL STREET SPIRIT-RAPPER

In 1887 the editor of *The Sheffield Telegraph,* described part of Ecclesall parish, lying between the General Cemetery at Sharrow and Bramhall Lane, as being 'rich in haunted houses and dwellings endowed with mysterious and fearsome noises'. The most sensational were those heard at Pearl Street in December 1881. The 'Pearl Street ghost' was recalled by Henry Tatton, who noted how, 'every night at a certain time there were mysterious knockings and the house used to shake; crowds congregated to hear the spirit knock, and many people were afraid to pass it at night'.

The haunted house was demolished during slum clearances in the 1960s that removed much of the Victorian housing in the Cemetery Road area of Sharrow. But in 1881 Sheffield's two daily papers published a series of reports on the activities of the 'spirit rapper'. These were based on evidence collected from tenants, some of whom had rented rooms in the back-to-back properties for 14 years.

The census of 1881, taken in April of that year, provides a snapshot of the families who lived in No 13 Court, Pearl Street, that became the focus of the alleged poltergeist. Many worked in the cutlery industry, either as grinders or table knife cutters.

A typical family was that of Joseph Hutchinson, 41, a file grinder who occupied a house in No 13 court with his wife Sarah Ann, 38, who was employed as a cutter.

They had four children including three daughters aged 19, 16 and 13 along with a son, aged 11. Late on the evening of 22 November one of the women raised the alarm when she heard the sound of someone 'knocking on the wall'. On asking around neighbours she discovered all had been disturbed by the same uncanny noises. From that day onwards the sounds continued daily without a break, firstly around noon and then just before 10 o'clock at night. This report, extracted from a lengthy article published by *The Sheffield Telegraph* on Thursday, 8 December 1881, provides colour to the mysterious happenings:

> **'In this practical age it is the custom to pooh-pooh ghosts and spirit rappers, but certain residents in Johnson's-yard, Pearl Street, off Sheffield-moor, are becoming convinced, like Hamlet, that supernatural beings are not such strangers to this world as some would imagine. Johnson's-yard is connected with Pearl Street by a narrow passage, on each side of which are two single houses. The occupants of these cottages have for the past week been greatly disturbed nightly by incessant knocking, the origin of which cannot be ascertained. It generally commences at ten o'clock, and goes on at intervals until midnight, and is making the people thereabouts very nervous and miserable.**

Pearl Street- site of the mysterious rappings, in 1965
PHOTO: Sheffield Libraries

Below: Newspaper coverage of the incident

"SPIRIT RAPPING" IN PEARL STREET.—For some few days past the neighbourhood of Pearl street has been thrown into a state of excitement by a rumour that "spirit rapping" had been heard in and about Johnson's yard, a court in that street. This has caused large crowds to assemble in the street each night, and has, in fact, caused considerable inconvenience and annoyance to persons resident there. Ten o'clock is the hour "arranged" for the "spirit" to carry on his rapping, and each night at this time hundreds of persons have congregated round the front of No. 13 court to await the phantom's appearance. On Thursday night it was rather disappointing; two or three thuds only were heard. Still this small performance satisfied the crowd, who were apparently prepared to remain in the cold all night, so long as the representative of Spirit Land was willing to knock. Whether some practical joker is at the

'At first it was thought that leaking water pipes were responsible for the methodical rapping, but on taking up the pavement it was ascertained that the pipes did not leak, and that the noise must have some other origin. The tapping is noticed more particularly in the lower rooms, and seems to arise from some industrious mechanic hammering away in the cellaring, but, as no one can possibly get into the cellars without the knowledge of the tenants, the belief is growing that some spirit is playing his pranks there with the intention of frightening people out of their wits. The ghost, or goblin, must have a very guilty conscience, and a very restless disposition, for he is scarcely ever quiet at night time, and turns up with his vigorous knocking in all sorts of odd places'.

Later on the day this story was published around one thousand people gathered in the street outside Johnson's-yard. *The Telegraph* said: '....gangs of youths prowled here and there, defying the spirit and daring the mysterious phantom to reveal himself. There was much noise and disorder, and hooting and groaning enough to terrify any ghost that retained an atom of self-respect'.

A reporter from *The Independent* who mingled with the crowd added: '...while some of the men and women who gathered in the street treated the knocking as a lark and an incident to be laughed at, others viewed the question very seriously and their faces, full of concern, indicated that they were not free from superstition.

'....gangs of youths prowled here and there, defying the spirit and daring the mysterious phantom to reveal himself.'

Pearl Street
Sheffield
Libraries

'The matrons are inclined to the opinion that the mysterious tapping was the forerunner of an earthquake. Various other explanations were hazarded as to the reason for the noises. One story was to the effect that a man, weary of this world and its troubles, had cut his throat by the fireside in some habitation near, and that his spirit was trying to find out his old haunts. Other stories equally absurd were brunted about, but obtained little credence'.

Whatever the cause of this rapping, the unruly crowd caused a great nuisance to one family that were most disturbed by the noises. The papers said one of the daughters of a grinder, Joseph Hodgkinson, (whose surname is spelled Hutchinson in the census) was 'lying seriously ill, and painfully irritated by the hubbub the thoughtless make about the cottage door'.

Police were summonsed to deal with the hubbub and four officers guarded the entrance to Johnsons-yard; 'they were obliged now and then to use their sticks, so unruly were some of the mob. One woman fainted, and many others were very terrified, but their terror arose quite as much from the conduct of the crowd as from any fear of the mysterious ghost'.

Worse was to come. One of those who joined the thousand-strong crowd was a 45-year-old midwife, Sarah Coldwell, who lived with her husband Edwin and two sons on Cemetery Road.

Onlookers said that as she waited for the spirit rappings to commence she suddenly put up her hand, exclaimed 'Oh my head', and then slumped unconscious to the floor. She was carried to a house on Pearl Street where a surgeon examined her and concluded 'she was suffering from apoplexy, the result, in all probability, of excitement and fright'.

Mrs Coldwell's condition worsened during the night and she died in Pearl Street the next day, without recovering consciousness. Her body was removed by undertakers in the evening 'in the sight of some waiting to hear the noises, and the rumour quickly spread that her death had been caused by the sounds'.

News of another 'death from fright' in the city was debunked by a report in *The Sheffield Telegraph*. This revealed how, two weeks before collapsing, the unfortunate lady had injured her head in a fall. A post-mortem examination found she died from what today would be called a stroke, but her death certificate records the cause as 'apoplexy'. Until the late 19th century this word was often used in cases where death was preceded by a sudden loss of consciousness.

One mystery was resolved but the source of the 'spirit rappings' continued to perplex the residents of Pearl Street. The weekend of 9-11 December brought more police to Johnson's-yard along with a 'scientific expert', Mr W.F. Cooper, who planned to install 'sensitive apparatus' in the the cellar of the haunted property.

1881.	Death in the Sub-district of Ecclesall Bierlow					in the County of York	
Columns:-	1	2	3	4	5	6	7
No.	When and where died	Name and surname	Sex	Age	Occupation	Cause of death	Signature, description and residence of informant
53	Ninth December 1881 71 Pearl Street Ecclesall Bierlow USD	Sarah Ann Coldwell	Female	45 years	Wife of Edwin Coldwell table knife forger	Apoplexy Certified by A H Laver MRCS	Edwin Coldwell Widower of deceased present at death 67 Duke Street Lane Sheffield

Sarah Coldwell's death certificate Sheffield Registry Office

Henry Tatton says many suspected miners '...whose workings were directly underneath the house'. No further rappings were heard until Sunday evening when 'four distinct thuds' were detected at 10 pm 'which could only be compared to those produced by the thump of a pavier's mallet when laying stones in the street'.

On Monday at noon the raps reappeared and continued for more than half an hour. The investigators returned to the cellar, 'with the most delicate instruments capable of detecting the slightest vibration, or the least display of magnetic or electrical currents. These were carefully scrutinised with a powerful lens, but not the slightest vibration or the least trace of a magnetic current could be detected'.

That evening hundreds of curious onlookers gathered outside the house, but were held back by five burly policemen. A reporter described the scene in the secluded cellar: 'in the company of a police officer, a Press man, and a solemn-looking hen perched on a beer barrel, [Mr Cooper] watched the needle to see which way it moved, so that he might decide if the mysterious sounds were caused by the "deflection of the earth's surfaces"'. As the hour of ten approached, someone exclaimed 'Here it goes!' and attention was suddenly concentrated on thuds which 'seemed to come from below the ground... four or six knocks were distinctly heard, and then the hammering ceased'.

Investigations quickly ruled out miners as the cause of the rappings. The houses were built over the Whinmoor coal, a very thin seam of coal , but this was not worked anywhere in the neighbourhood of Pearl Street; 'neither were the houses linked to the main sewer, except by surface drainage'. Oddly, the rappings were much louder in the room above the cellar. They appeared to vary in intensity 'being louder at times when, from the density of the air they should theoretically be less distinct'.

LOCAL INTELLIGENCE.

THE PEARL STREET "SPIRIT RAPPING."—A number of people, though not so many as on previous occasions, assembled in Pearl street last evening to hear "the rapper" at work, but only met with disappointment, for no unusual noises were heard. The afflicted little girl who has, by public rumour, been associated with the rappings, was removed to a sofa in the lower room.

THE SPIRIT RAPPER IN PEARL STREET.—Last evening the usual crowd assembled in Pearl street for the purpose of hearing the Pearl street spirit rapper ... its customary ten o'clock operations. Unfor... the crowd there also appeared Detective-...nack, of the Highfield division, and his ...must evidently have surmised that that officer was "on the spot," for both the the rapping were unseen and unheard. It ...rhaps, also in justice be remembered that . Cooper was present, for the purpose of con...is investigation, which he has been good ...n carry on. The little girl who has been poorly ...ned to her bed was able to be removed down-...a short time last night, and it is to be hoped that her recovery towards convalescence will not be interfered with by any further repetition of the practical joke, which the "jokists" themselves must now admit is played out. It is singular perhaps that the cessation of the knocking should be simultaneous with the little girl coming downstairs. That is a point

All the experts agreed the weight of evidence pointed to a practical joke, but by whom? If it was a prank, mused the *Telegraph*, it was a cruel one as the young daughter of Mr Hutchinson 'is slowly dying with a brain disease and during her conscious intervals she is much annoyed by the lads climbing up to the window to look in to see the ghost'. The writer added: 'I have visited the "haunted house" repeatedly [and]...it is an utter impossibility for the sick child to rise from her bed. It would be impossible for a child paralysed as she is to lift a hammer and to produce these sounds'.

At the weekend Detective-officer Womack and Inspector Jacob Bradbury, of the Highfield division, arrived in Pearl Street. They were determined to lay the 'ghost'. Bradbury was described by the *Telegraph* 'as the shrewdest man in the [Sheffield] police force' (see pg 89). One of the journalists assigned to the story noticed how on Tuesday, 14 December 'the little girl who has been poorly and confined to her bed was able to be removed downstairs for a short time last night' and he added: 'it is singular perhaps that the cessation of the knocking should be simultaneous with the little girl coming downstairs. That is a point which might admit of inquiry'.

By now street rumours were linking the little girl with the strange rappings and Inspector Bradbury was growing suspicious.

On the night of Wednesday, 15 December, he instructed Sergeant Swift to stand guard near the room where the 'poor dying girl...lay upon the sofa' so as 'to be in communication with his superior' when the rappings began. Ten o'clock came and went, but nothing unusual was heard and by 10.45 the crowd outside had given up and dispersed. At 11.10 the police officers slipped away and within half an hour 'the rappings were heard both loud and deep'.

What happened next required a bit of detective work of my own. As of 17 December 1881 nothing further was heard from the Pearl Street ghost, at least not in the pages of Sheffield's newspapers. But six years later *The Telegraph* admitted that whilst its reporters were holed up in the cellar with the scientist, 'a little lass was amusing herself upstairs, and half the people in the neighbourhood were frightened out of their wits – several of them out of their houses – while hundreds came from all parts of the town to stare at the bricks and mortar that contained the mystery'.

The newspaper credited Inspector Bradbury with having 'laid the Pearl Street ghost' in the following manner: he 'took it into his head to mount guard at a certain house, where he discovered the knocking was done by a meek-faced female of tender years, supposed to be too weak to clang anything against a wall'.

POLICING THE PARANORMAL

LAYING A GHOST AT CHESTERFIELD. 'The other night a policeman was stationed in the churchyard for the purpose of protecting the church from the evil-disposed... A brother officer, wishing to indulge in a 'lark', procured a sheet, and having covered himself with it, he took up position in one of the porches, which the officer on duty would have to pass. In a few moments Mr Policeman arrived, and out jumped the 'ghost'. The officer was for a moment startled, but on recovering his wits he dealt the man in white a blow with his stick. 'Alas poor ghost!' he was glad to make his exit as speedily as possible for fear the chastisement would be repeated.' *Sheffield & Rotherham Independent, 20 April 1867*

Sheffield's police force came into existence shortly before Queen Victoria's reign began. In 1818 Col Thomas Fenton was appointed as superintendent of just 23 men, a tiny number by modern standards, but at that time Sheffield was just a small town. He was succeeded in 1836 by Thomas Raynor as chief inspector and a regular day force was formed. These doubled up as night-watchmen in a zone around the parish church, but remained few in number.

With the industrial revolution in full swing, an organised and efficient crime-fighting force was needed and from 1843 the police came under the control of the town council's Watch Committee. Soon afterwards, the numbers were increased to cope with the Chartist movement.

In 1839 their leader, Samuel Holberry, was personally arrested by the Chief Constable during a riot in the town centre. He was imprisoned at York Castle and after ill treatment died, age 27, in 1842. Thousands turned out to give him a martyr's funeral when his body was brought to rest in Sheffield's General Cemetery.

By 1855, when police were called to disperse disorderly crowds gathered outside the 'haunted house' on Campo Lane, the strength of the force had increased to 122 men. This included an inspector, three sergeants, a clerk and 28 constables.

There was also a night force and even a small detective section. Detectives were a novelty at the time but were celebrated in fiction by Charles Dickens and Wilkie Collins. Possibly the most celebrated detective of the era was Jack Whicher of Scotland Yard. His investigation of the murder of a three-year -old boy at Road Hill House in 1860 was subject of a best-selling book by Kate Summerscale, *The Suspicions of Mr Whicher* (2008) that was adapted into a television drama.

Inspector Jacob Bradbury, whom we met earlier in this chapter, was Sheffield's answer to Jack Whicher. The two men were active during the middle of the 19th century and both had working class backgrounds. Bradbury joined the force as a probationer in 1849, the year in which the first English detective story, written by journalist William Russell, was published by *Chambers's Edinburgh Journal.*

Dickens was a fan of the clever, plain-clothed detectives and in creating the character Inspector Bucket for *Bleak House* (1853) he summarised their appearance and qualities. There was nothing mysterious about Bucket except his 'ghostly manner of appearing'. He was '...a stoutly built, steady-looking, sharp-eyed man in black' who watched and listened for clues.

Although there is no surviving description or even a photograph of Inspector Bradbury, I have been able to piece together a profile of his busy life in Sheffield's embryonic police force. During the 19th century the force were based at the Old Town Hall on Waingate (the former Crown Court building).

Chief Constable
John Jackson
Sheffield Libraries

By 1859 when a new Chief Constable, John Jackson, arrived in Sheffield, Bradbury had been promoted from constable to sergeant. In 1864 he was one of a small group of policemen who were rewarded by the Watch Committee for 'extraordinary diligence and exertion in saving life and property' after the bursting of the Bradfield dam left hundreds dead and homeless in the town centre. Bradbury's entry in Sheffield Police personnel records contains details of three other 'rewards and gratuities for meritorious conduct' received during a career that spanned half a century. Bradbury became an inspector in 1869 and in that year he had one of his first experiences policing a 'ghost alarm'. During the summer rumours spread about a haunted house at the corner of Button Lane and Eldon Street, near The Moor. A report in *The Sheffield Telegraph* of 13 August told how 'a large crowd... collected before a gloomy looking building which, it was said, had not been occupied for a considerable space of time'. Two children, who had entered the house to play, fled after being terrified by the sight of 'something in white' and quickly told their story to people outside who 'lost no time in circulating an exaggerated version' to all and sundry. Great excitement was generated and a crowd of people gathered outside the 'haunted house'. By the time Bradbury's men arrived the windows had been shattered by the mob and 'a general cry arose to enter the upper story, but those who were so valorous outside could not pluck up enough courage...and instead contented themselves by firing volleys of stones'. It was an old belief that loud noises could scare away spirits and so the crowd took to 'shouting at the top of their voices, to frighten it away'.

The crowd of 600 was eventually dispersed by half a dozen constables, but people continued to return to scene for several days. Reports in *The Telegraph* imply the police used heavy-armed tactics to deal with some of the more unruly elements among the crowds. One young woman was left unconscious after witnesses claimed she was kicked by a constable whilst 'satisfying a little idle and harmless curiosity' by visiting the haunted house whilst on her way home from work. Soon afterwards a young man, George Turton, was fined one shilling after he was found guilty of obstructing the footpath in Button Lane.

Scared To Death

Illustrated Police News, 1878. The Escape and capture of Charles Peace

In court, he was described as a having created a great disturbance but 'the defendant denied that he had been ordered to "move on" and said that the officer, without saying anything to him, struck him in the mouth'.

Violence in the street and in the home was common throughout the Victorian age and police officers often became the target of such attacks. In 1873 two constables were treated for serious head injuries after being struck by stones hurled by the street ruffians who gathered at Clay Wood quarry during the hunt for the Park Ghost (see pg 62). By that time Bradbury had taken charge of the newly-formed Highfield division that covered a large semi-rural area consisting of present day Ecclesall Road, Sharrow and Woodseats.

It was during this time that he was to be drawn into some of the most exciting investigations of his career. These included forensic work that led to the arrest of a young housekeeper, Kate Dover, for the murder of a 62-year-old widower, Thomas Skinner, of Glover Road, Lowfield. The pair fell ill after eating a chicken stuffed with herbs, but Dover, 26, survived. When she was arrested she exclaimed: 'How could you think I could do such a thing?' but at the coroner's inquest it emerged that she had bought arsenic the day before the meal. She was convicted of murder at Leeds Assizes in 1882 and was sentenced to penal servitude for life.

By far the most famous case in Bradbury's entire career was 'the Banner Cross murder'. On 29 November 1876, a Sheffield-born burglar and house breaker, Charles Peace, shot and killed a retired railway engineer, Arthur Dyson, outside his home on Banner Cross Terrace. Dyson had recently moved there from Darnall to escape Peace who had grown fond of his wife Kathryn. It was this crime of passion that brought an end to Peace's long career as 'the King of Burglars'.

As Dyson's murder occurred in the Highfield division, Inspector Bradbury was immediately placed in charge of the investigation. Shortly afterwards posters were circulated offering a reward of £100 for Peace's capture. Peace was a master of disguise and, using a series of aliases, he slipped out of Bradbury's clutches and escaped first to Hull and then to Nottingham before embarking on a burglary spree across England. According to the legend that grew up around Peace, on one occasion his disguise was so convincing that, on returning to Sheffield, he walked past Bradbury in the street without being recognised. Peace's fabled agility and luck in evading capture ran out in October 1878 when he was caught red-handed breaking into a house in London. At the end of his trial at Leeds Town Hall in February, 1879, he was found guilty of Dyson's murder and sentenced to death.

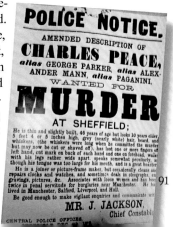

POLICE NOTICE.

AMENDED DESCRIPTION OF

CHARLES PEACE,

alias GEORGE PARKER, *alias* ALEX-ANDER MANN, *alias* PAGANINI,

WANTED FOR

MURDER

AT SHEFFIELD;

He is thin and slightly built, 46 years of age but looks 10 years older, 5 feet 4 or 5 inches high, grey (nearly white) hair, beard, and whiskers, (the whiskers were long when he committed the murder but may now be cut or shaved off), has lost one or more fingers of left hand, cut mark on back of each hand and one on forehead, walks with his legs rather wide apart, speaks somewhat peculiarly, as though his tongue was too large for his mouth, and is a great boaster. He is a joiner or picture-frame maker, but occasionally cleans and repairs clocks and watches, and sometimes deals in oleographs, engravings, pictures, &c. Associates with loose women and has been twice in penal servitude for burglaries near Manchester. He has lived in Manchester, Salford, Liverpool, and Hull.

Be good enough to make vigilant enquiries and communicate with

MR. J. JACKSON,
Chief Constable

CENTRAL POLICE OFFICES,

Inspector Bradbury must have been relieved to know that his nemesis Peace had met his end for the murder of Dyson on his patch. But this would have been tempered by frustration that it was the Metropolitan police, and not the officers in his home town, who were responsible for bringing him to justice.

Nevertheless, on his retirement in March 1896 *The Sheffield Telegraph*, in its tribute to the 70-year-old Bradbury, said he had served 45 years and two months in the force and 'during his long service the retiring inspector has earned the respect of those with whom he has come in contact as a steady and reliable officer. He has indeed become known by the venerable title of "father of the force"'. The newspaper mentioned another, lesser known, reputation that Bradbury had acquired during his years as one of Sheffield's shrewdest detectives. He had become a cool-headed ghostbuster. The elderly detective was 'a scourge of apparitions and won't let a poor ghost live in his division... [he] was instrumental in discovering the deception practised on the credulous in the Pearl Street ghost mystery some years ago'. Four years before his retirement Bradbury's ghost-laying skills were called upon for one last time to investigate a haunting at the Brunswick Methodist chapel, which once stood on South Street, The Moor. Late in October 1892 'a figure in a white sheet' was seen pacing between the windows late at night. As had become customary, 'a small crowd has congregated each week-evening in front of the building'.

Within days the *Telegraph* reported how the ghost had been 'laid' by Bradbury who discovered 'the chapel ghost turned out to be a big poster on the lobby notice board. It had got loose and flapped about, its flappings being visible to the naked eyes of outsiders. Hence the "mysterious visions" and "the white sheet"'!

Brunswick Chapel, Inspector Bradbury's last case
Sheffield Libraries

When Chief Constable John Jackson retired in the summer of 1896 he referred, in his speech, to Inspector Bradbury, as being the 'the last and most venerable member of the original Sheffield police force' of 177 that existed when he took charge in 1859. Bradbury was pensioned with an allowance of £6 13s 4d. per month but did not live to enjoy it. Two months after suffering a stroke, Inspector Jacob Bradbury died at his daughter's home on Sharrow Lane, Ecclesall, on 28 August 1897. He was 71 years old.

7
IMPERSONATING GHOSTS

'...from time immemorial there have been foolish persons who have affected to play the part of a ghost. In the days of yore, when superstition was supreme, the nocturnal disturbers, who stalked about with solemn pride, were supposed to be supernatural, and affrighted all whom they approached; but in these modern times when Materialism finds such favour, ghosts are at a discount. Sometimes one puts in an appearance in a country place; but he has to be very careful in his movements, because every human being does not recede from him in fear...'

This editorial, published by *The Daily Gazette* in September 1879, was written in response to the craze for 'ghost impersonation' that was widespread in Britain during the Victorian period. Newspapers reported many scares in lonely places often on the edges of urban areas where outbreaks were particularly common during the winter months.

Historian Jacob Middleton, who has collected examples from the Victorian media, says although few people believed these 'ghosts' were restless spirits, they produced 'a general atmosphere of fear and apprehension' in rural communities as they exploited older, deep-rooted supernatural beliefs. As a result, as night fell the old and vulnerable locked themselves in their homes, while others assembled in gangs and armed themselves with weapons to indulge in ghost-hunting expeditions.

Park Head, Ecclesall, scene of a
mistaken attack on a 'ghost.'
Sheffield Libraries

In some cases the vigilantes who joined such spontaneous gatherings were prepared to take the law into their own hands. When 'ghosts' were identified or captured they could face summary justice at the hands of the mob. In a few cases this could result in death. The most tragic case occurred in north London when, in January 1804, a brick-layer, Thomas Milward, was shot dead by an Excise Officer, Francis Smith, who believed he was the 'Hammersmith ghost' that plagued the neighbourhood dressed in a white sheet. He was found guilty of murder and sentenced to death, but this was subsequently reduced and eventually he received a pardon from the king.

In 1857 a Derbyshire man was tried for manslaughter following the death from fright of a 15-year-old boy, Robert Mitchell, in Alfreton. A jury at Derby Assizes heard that Mitchell was in the habit of fetching milk from a farm via a path that had a reputation for being haunted. One morning in December 1856, a servant on the farm, John Percival, decided to play a joke on the teenager by donning a white sheet, then 'took his station by a stile on the footpath by which the deceased would re-turn home'. On reaching home the victim of the prank looked 'pale and frightened'. The following morning he collapsed and 'died in a state of great exhaustion'. Mitchell was found not guilty and freed, but was warned by the judge 'never again to indulge in practical jokes'.

The death of Hannah Rallison 'from fright' following an encounter with a white lady ghost in a cellar in Campo Lane, Sheffield, in 1855 was not blamed on a ghost impersonator, but some preferred to believe she had been duped by pranksters using a magic lantern to project ghostly images on the wall of the building (see pg 22).

By the later Victorian period fear of the supernatural appeared to be in decline as social attitudes towards ghosts began to change. Street-lighting and policing were an added deterrent for the assorted men – young and old - who enjoyed impersonating ghosts. Nevertheless, in 1887 the editors of Sheffield's newspapers expressed sur-prise that even in these enlightened times 'there are some people who still believe in ghosts... Particular districts of town have now and again been credited with possessing ghosts of a mischief-loving turn of mind, and many worthy souls have in consequence been frightened pretty well out of their wits'.

Shortly before Christmas of that year a ghost scare spread across the town, affecting both urban Broomhill, where 'Spring-heeled Jack' was on the prowl, (see pg 67) and rural Ecclesall. Coincidentally, 'Miss E. Smith's Original Pepper's Ghost' show was in residence at the Music Hall, Surrey Street, and was drawing large crowds. The show was an adaptation of Charles Dickens' *A Christmas Carol*, featuring Fred Smith as Ebenezer Scrooge. It was followed by a 'grand concert, in which Miss Emily Cameron and Mr Harry West took part, and the whole concluded with a laughable spectral farce'.

TO NIGHT, AT 6 AND 8.
NEW VESTRY HALL, WESTBAR.
(On the site of the old Surrey Theatre.)
THIS EVENING AND EVERY EVENING
DURING THE HOLIDAYS, CHARLES DICKENS'
CHRISTMAS CAROL,
With all the Marvellous Spectacle Effects, Phantoms, Ghosts, Spirits, Angels, &c., by Professor PEPPER'S GHOST ILLUSION.
In order that Parents may be able to bring their Children to the Entertainment there will be an Early Performance at Six o'Clock each Evening, when Children will be admitted at Half-price to all parts. Admission: Sixpence and Threepence.

For one Sheffield gentleman the subject of ghosts was to prove anything but a subject of mirth. At that time Park Head, Ecclesall Road South, consisted a scattering of cottages. The Park Head ghost was 'said to haunt the road between the Mr Charles Belk's residence and the Wheat Sheaf Inn, kept by Mr Philip Vardy'. In the early hours of 21 December a retired businessman, George Chapman, set out from his home at Broomhill. He intended to walk 20 miles to the farm he owned in Eyam, Derbyshire, a trip he made on foot, dressed in top hat and overcoat, at least once a week. What happened next is best explained by the court proceedings that followed at Sheffield Town Hall. Versions of the case were published by the *Sheffield Telegraph* and the *Sheffield & Rotherham Independent,* on Thursday, 29 December 1887:

THE COURT PROCEEDINGS

Jacob Bradwell, Richard Broomhead and Joseph Ellis, of Ecclesall, appeared on a summons that charged them with having assaulted George Chapman, of Durham Road. Mr Muir Wilson appeared for the complainant, and Mr Fairburn for Ellis. Mr Wilson, in stating the case, said the complainant was retired from business, and owned a farm at Eyam. He was walking there last Wednesday morning at 7 o'clock when the assault took place. He was alone and on reaching a place known as Bents Green Road he suddenly came across the defendant, Jacob Bradwell, who threw a bottle at him.

Mr Fairburn: 'He was going to lay the ghost I suppose!' (Laughter).

Mr Wilson: 'The defendant had evidently mistaken Mr Chapman for the ghost, but this was no excuse for such an attack. The bottle actually struck Mr Chapman on the hand, and then Bradwell ran away as fast as he could. Mr Chapman ran after him, thinking it was an escaped lunatic who had attacked him, and got to the post office where he inquired after Bradwell. The post office was kept by Mr Ellis. When he was telling him what had taken place Bradwell came up and said, pointing to Mr Chapman: 'Who's that man? Turn him out'. Ellis went into his house, which was close by, and fetched out a large stick. Bradwell went away, but returned in a very short time accompanied by Broomhead. The latter shook Mr Chapman, and told him 'Oh yes, you have been a terror to the neighbourhood for a long time, you have been frightening all the children out of their wits, and we'll pay you off this time'. One said 'Produce the mask!' but Mr Chapman replied that he had not got one. He tried to reason with the three defendants, who held him by the shoulder.

Mr Chapman, an elderly man, was then called. He said last Wednesday was a dark and foggy morning when he set out. He then described the defendant Bradwell's extraordinary attack.

He had no such thing as a mask on, He said Bradwell came close up to him, but the bottle did not strike him in the face, although that was where Bradwell aimed. ►

THE COURT PROCEEDINGS Continued

Mr Wilson: 'Have you done anything to cause him to do that? Had you been wearing a mask or anything of that kind?'

Complainant: 'No, I've never had one in my life to my knowledge'.

Giving evidence, Jacob Bradwell said as he was going to his work he suddenly saw someone standing against the wall. He said 'hello' but got no answer. He walked a little further on, and came close to the individual, who stepped off the causeway and 'stared right in his face'. The man had a big topcoat and a big top hat on and was disguised, wearing, he believed, a mask on his face. He spoke to him again, but still got no reply and, merely out of fright, he shook his breakfast can at him. He emphatically denied throwing the can at the complainant.

Broomhead stated that his nephew Bradwell had only left the house five minutes when he returned in a frightened state. He thought Bradwell would drop down dead (laughter) because he was troubled with heart disease. He (Broomhead) said: 'Whatever is amiss lad?' and he replied: 'Ghost, ghost!'. The old man followed Bradwell with a stick. He (Broomhead) got hold of Chapman and shook him and called him an old scamp for having acted the ghost and frightened women and children in the neighbourhood.

Mr Fairburn, on behalf of Ellis, said his client saw Chapman looking very much like a ghost, and so far from assaulting him was there to protect him. As a matter of fact, Ellis chased Bradwell, whom he thought to be the ghost. It was as wretched and trumpery a case as the Bench ever had before it.

The Bench dismissed the case.

Mr Fairburn: I hope this will practically 'lay the ghost'.

Mr Wilson:' I hope my client will now have peace, but old men should be protected from outrage when they are walking along a road'.

The Wheatsheaf, Park Head
Sheffield Libraries

RAISING "A GHOST" AT ECCLESALL.

AN EXTRAORDINARY MISTAKE.

For some time past there has been a ghost scare at Park Head, Ecclesall. The residents thereabouts, or at least some of them, are under the delusion that a ghostly visitant may be seen taking his walks abroad and that his favourite place for thus exercising his fleshless bones is the high road from the Wheat Sheaf to the residence of Mr. Charles Belk. It is, of course, unnecessary to say that no one has seen the ... and therefore, accounts differ as to what ... more or less ... the powe... ing whatever... hole thing i... hese last year... ne people wh... which occurred... o means amu... man, who live... in Derbyshire... alk there fron... morning. He... hour afterward... s Sheat public... forgry, and the...

MISTAKING A SHEFFIELD GENTLEMAN FOR A GHOST.

EXTRAORDINARY DELUSION AT PARK HEAD.

Particular districts of Sheffield have now and again been credited with possessing ghosts of a mischievous turn of mind, and many worthy souls have in consequence been frightened pretty well out of their wits. It is a long time since one of these ghost scares occupied public attention; but at Park Head, Ecclesall matters unpleasant for several days. This ghost is said to haunt the road between Mr. Charles Belk's residence and the Wheat Sheaf Inn kept by Mr. Philip Vardy. In what shap...

'Spectator in Hallamshire', writing in the columns of *The Sheffield & Rotherham Independent* on New Year's Eve, 1887, said he believed most people would conclude that, 'in the gloom of a foggy winter's morning, both of the men were in dire funk, and so absurdly alarmed at one another that they acted rather irrationally'. But 'Spectator' believed it was 'a little curious' how persistent ghost traditions were in the area around Bents Green. And he continued to share a few with the paper's readers: 'There is the story of a phantom dog (a black retriever) which haunts the road near where Bradwell incontinently flung his breakfast can at the unghostly Chapman's head. And some quarter of a mile off, above Broad Oak, is the scene of the celebrated spectral equipage of Bent's Green.

'Have I not told you the story before? Briefly it is this: Bent's Green Lodge, best known as a the residence of the late Mr Albert Smith, was originally the Rising Sun public house [built in 1787 by Lord John Murray]. One day the land-

...the old-fashioned chariot, with lamps lit, and the two clergymen seated inside, has been seen to come driving out of Bent's Green gates and over the scene of the murder.

lord, in a passion, killed a carter at the corner of the lane leading to Whiteley Wood, by knocking him off the shaft, when the wheel ran over his head. The crime was not discovered, but on his deathbed the murderer, oppressed by remorse, desired to relieve his soul by confession, and sent for the Rev George Smith, curate of Ecclesall. As the Rev James Wilkinson, Vicar and Justice of the Peace, was that day taking duty at Ecclesall Church, the two clergymen drove to Bent's Green together in the vicar's coach and there received the dying man's confession.

'And occasionally, late at night, the old-fashioned chariot, with lamps lit, and the two clergymen seated inside, has been seen to come driving out of Bent's Green gates and over the scene of the murder. The late Mr Blakelock Smith used to declare that, riding home late one night, after a long day at Eckington Sessions, he encountered the phantom equipage driving out of the gates, and, determined to see his grandfather if possible, he put spurs to his horse and galloped after. But before he could overtake it the carriage went round the corner, and there it disappeared.

'I assure my incredulous readers that the equipage has also been seen by other credible witnesses – at least they say so. As the approach to Bent's Green Lodge has been altered, and the old gates walled up, I presume the spectral carriage has been exorcised. At any rate, my strong desire to encounter it, in many nocturnal visits to the scene of its activities, has never been gratified'.

Bents Green Lodge
Sheffield
Libraries

'...No more likely spot could have been selected for the wanderings of a ghost, especially if he be of a philosophic cast of mind and would delight in drawing gloomy comparisons between the old village and the modern...It is not many years since this prosperous little place was yet unreclaimed country, and green lanes and hills yet surround the grimy dwellings wherein the workmen of the district live. Grass fields and wooded ways are yet to be found on the outskirts, and the situation of the curiously-grouped dwellings, the modern mingled promiscuously with the ancient, renders it decidedly picturesque...' *Sheffield and Rotherham Independent* 14 January 1896

THE BRIGHTSIDE GHOST SCARE.—Never was a ghost so intangible as the spirit which is said to be haunting the north-eastern districts of the city and suburbs. It is absolutely impossible for the searchers to get a sight of it, and yet there are constant stories of its appearance. Pitsmoor and Brightside are in a state of great perturbation. Women decline to go out after nightfall, unless escorted, and all the children are scared. The police incline to the belief that there is nothing whatever in the stories which are circulated, and are unable to find anybody who has absolutely seen anything. But, on the other hand, the residents are persistent in their declarations that the statements in circulation are based on fact. Probably, not half a dozen in all the district could be found who think that the apparition is a supernatural being. There is too much commonsense for that notion to prevail nowadays, but its appearance is nevertheless said to justify all the fears that are entertained. The rumour is now in circulation in the district that the ghost has been walking to win a wager, that the period over which the foolhardy exploit was to extend terminated on Friday night, and that the spectre will be no more seen. If there has been any appearance it may be hoped that this rumour is true; and if the whole scare has been due to a wicked invention in the first instance, and a too vivid and quick imagination afterwards, it may be further hoped that it will subside, for several painful contretemps are reported, one especially, in which one searcher has injured another rather badly under the belief that he

Wincobank Hill
PHOTO: The author

8
THE BRIGHTSIDE GHOST

By the end of Queen Victoria's long reign the village of Brightside had become the central focus for the heavy industry that dominated the lives of everyone who lived in Sheffield's East End. Steelworks and huge factories were spread along the banks of the River Don and new roads, shops and rows of terraced houses were built to cope with the demands of the growing workforce. Yet despite the creeping industrialisation, rural areas of the valley retained a wild and eerie reputation.

Earlier in the 19th century visitors to Sheffield who passed through Attercliffe Common would have noticed a gibbet post beside the road. From the post dangled the remains of a highwayman, Spence Broughton. He was hanged at York in 1792 for holding up the Sheffield & Rotherham mail coach and, as was the custom at that time, his body was exhibited at the scene of his crime. It was estimated that 40,000 people turned out to see the grisly spectacle and parts of Broughton's skeleton were much in demand as ghoulish ornaments. The gibbet post remained standing until 1827 when it was removed by a farmer.

Throughout the Victorian century fear of meeting the restless spirit of Spence Broughton must have plagued those whose business took them to Attercliffe Common during the hours of darkness. Two weeks before Christmas in 1895 stories began to spread about the antics of a mysterious ghost that prowled the lonely hillsides between Brightside and the ancient Iron Age earthworks on Wincobank hill and nearby Roman Rig. Like a highwayman, the apparition preyed upon solitary travellers 'in the guise of a tall cloaked figure robed in white, with a deathlike face and strange head-dress...it never spoke, and silently melted in the air'.

The panic began late at night on a lonely lane near the hamlet of Osgathorpe. A young lady 'was accosted by a tall and dark-lined figure attired, apparently, in a large and enveloping red cloak'. Naturally petrified, she turned to flee, but froze when she saw the 'ghost' throw the cloak from his shoulders, disclosing a ghostly white costume. Worse was to come: 'His face then appeared to become illuminated by a phosphorescent glare, and the exhibition was brought to a close by the spirit solemnly and with measured strides – walking backwards!'

Artists impression of Attercliffe Common at the close of the 18th century, showing Arrow Inn, Carbrook Hall and Broughton's gibbet **Sheffield Libraries**

The woman ran back home to report her strange experience and before long the question 'have you seen the ghost?' was being asked on every street. *The Sheffield Telegraph* said her story generated a 'feeling of dread' amongst residents of Brightside, Pitsmoor and Grimesthorpe 'and even at the smallest trifle, not only women, but also youths and even men, run as for dear life'.

Initially the phantom confined his activities to the hillsides but by the New Year, Brightside village itself was visited. A resident of Dearne Street, Mr Short, returning home at a late hour, saw the apparition 'cloaked...and with face glaring in the moving light, standing silently in his path...the same incomprehensible backward-stepping movements were repeated, and the phantom disclosed the white vesture enveloping him in a manner now grown familiar'. Mr Short appeared to have had the best view as he noticed the ghost was wearing peculiar headgear consisting of 'white feathers'.

A third close encounter was reported by a young butcher from Brightside who met the 'ghost' in a secluded lane. In this case, 'in an unfrequented lane, at a little distance from Brightside proper, the well-known figure sprang as if from the bowels of the earth'.

...the ghost had made a poor choice of victim as this youth was armed with one of the tools of his trade - a meat cleaver!

But the ghost had made a poor choice of victim as this youth was armed with one of the tools of his trade - a meat-cleaver ! He raised the weapon, 'with the intention of testing the materiality of the spirit's substance [but]...before the blow could descend, the shade turned on his heel with human promptness, and vanished into darkness'.

The identity of the 'Brightside ghost' was subject to fevered discussion. Had Spence Broughton returned? Or was this another visit from the Park Ghost, Spring-heeled Jack? The white costume suggested shrouds in which dead bodies were buried and Daniel Defoe, writing in 1727, said that apparitions were expected to appear 'dressed up...as if they had just come out of a coffin and the churchyard'. White sheets were also popular with those who enjoyed impersonating ghosts and *The Sheffield Telegraph* noted that many were of the opinion '...that the trick is a wager on the part of some person attired in white, and wearing in addition a dark overcoat lined with white material...but when the overcoat is fastened he passes muster as an ordinary traveller, and on meeting with women or persons likely to be frightened, he unfastens the coat and performs antics. Some allege that he carries a lamp which he skilfully flashes on his own countenance and adds to its ghastliness'.

The paper reported a feeling 'amounting almost to terror' had spread amongst the inhabitants, 'the female and youthful section being particularly alarmed. It became almost dangerous to walk abroad in the night time, and those afflicted with nerves were wont to gaze around them, as if expecting an apparition to start from every bridge, or emerge from every tree-thrown shadow'.

The police did their best to reassure the population there was 'nothing whatever in the stories which are circulated' but said they were 'unable to find anybody who has absolutely seen anything'. The paper added: 'The other night the constable on duty at Osgathorpe was astonished to hear the pattering of feet, and to find a young man rush into his arms. This individual, having partly regained his breath, explained that he and a friend had seen the ghost, and had both bolted, though in different directions. This was the constable's opportunity, and he took the frightened youth back along the path to search for the spook. A short distance on they came upon a venerable old man, with a long grey beard, dressed in white corduroys, who explained that as he was walking along he met two young men, who had promptly run away as if mad, and he had been waiting to see what had frightened them. He himself had come to escort home a young relative who was afraid of tramping the fields alone'.

Inevitably, scenes similar to those that followed the appearance of the 'Park Ghost' in 1873 were repeated: '...several gangs of men and youths and other small parties have been out at night to lay the ghost', some armed with six-shooters and bulldogs, 'and he may depend on a warm reception when caught'.

Wincobank Hill
Sheffield Libraries

In a little distance from Brightside proper, the well-known figure sprang as if from the bowels of the earth

One shopkeeper decorated his window with a notice reading: 'Physic for the Bright-side Ghost – Swordsticks, 1s 6d each' and soon life became dangerous for anyone walking the streets whilst dressed in white. One hapless factory worker, 'taking his usual stroll in quest of supper-beer...was unceremoniously cuffed by a party of ardent ghost-hunters who, deceived by the glamour of the white overalls, thought they had alighted upon the object of their search. No one came to the assistance of the surprised and discomfited workman, and his cries for mercy died away upon the midnight air'.

On 24 January, 1896, *The Sheffield & Rotherham Independent* declared the Bright-side ghost 'was still at large'. It reported that 'either the ghost is doing a vast amount of travelling, or has related its experiences to other spirits who have their habitation near the smoky city' because every district of Sheffield had now acquired a 'Bright-side ghost' of its own. Attercliffe, Darnall, Sharrow, Heeley and Endcliffe had all been visited by the 'being from the other world' and it had wandered across the border into neighbouring Rotherham with sightings reported at Kimberworth, Clifton Park and Gerard Road.

During the scare a journalist on *The Sheffield Independent* wrote that 'what-ever his ultimate fate the ghost will undoubtedly leave a deep impression in the recollections of dwellers in the district'. And sure enough, half a centu-ry later the scare was recalled by an interview in *The Sheffield Star*. In 1955 Joe Somerfield, then aged 69, recalled how 'sixty years ago', during his childhood in the 1890s, 'a character called Spring-heeled Jack' or 'the Brightside ghost' had terrorised the neighbourhood of Heeley and had become a local legend. 'They never caught him but people were so scared they never forgot him', he said.

Somerfield's account was just one of many rumours about a ghostly prowler, of-ten referred to as 'Spring-heeled Jack', in the Attercliffe and Pitsmoor districts of Sheffield during the early 20th century. According to my grandfather, on one occasion during the 1920s he was spotted, appropriately, jumping along the roof of the Tempest Spring Company in Attercliffe. He took a giant leap from the roof, scaring workers. Another story, this time from my paternal great-grandmother, told of Spring-heeled Jack pursued by policemen in Pitsmoor, where the family lived during the First World War: 'He was cornered in Burngreave Cemetery and jumped over the huge cemetery gates to escape from the crowd that were chasing him'.

As recently as the mid-1970s stories were circulated about 'the prowler of Westbury Street', who terrorised residents of Attercliffe. In a web article linking the prowler to the legend of Spring-heeled Jack, Sheffield author Martin Jeffrey quotes anonymous informants from Attercliffe. One describes a figure jumping across rooftops, taking huge bounds of twenty to thirty feet. Another described the figure as '....very tall, six feet six inches at least, dressed in black...he also had a black cape, but his face I can't remember, just those burning red eyes; I honestly think he was the Devil'.

NED FLATBACK'S GHOST

Mr Jacob Bradall's Narrative To His Friends

This story appeared in the Christmas supplement of *The Sheffield Daily Telegraph* on 29 December, 1877. It is reproduced here in its original dialect form.

Tell thee a tale? Aye, to be sure. I reckon you'd like something with a moral to it? (The company assented).

Well, then, it's often been on my mind to speak of a personal adventure with a ghost – not of a spring-heel'd imposter like that which frightened so many folks in the Park some years ago; nor like that rattletoppin' scamp that caused such a row in Campo-lane a while since.

No, what I'm bound to speak of was a quiet, decent sort of ghost, that harm'd nobody but myself. You must know, then, that Rumour said that my old friend and fellow-worker, Ned Flatback, couldn't rest in his last long home, but that he roam'd about his old house at nights, and nobody would live in it. Whether his conscience troubled him because he'd not paid all his natty-money and had left the world in debt, or whether he'd paid too much, I cannot say.

However, they said he was restless and haunted the home of his ancestors. Well, there was a meeting one night of the Aletasters' Union (Barrel Inn branch) at which the subject came up. I was there, and astonished the weakly nervous by offering to sleep in the house any night they'd a mind – that is, if I could have fair play and no practical joking.

The company were delighted at my proposal. The chairman (Thomas Raandhead, Esq.) thought that in the interests of science, and as contributing to their social enjoyment, and as no doubt Mr Bradall's midnight mission would go far to expose the bunkum about Spiritualism, he hoped their friend would not withdraw from his offer.

And so I agreed.

Well, the preliminaries and the night were fixed upon. I was to sleep in Ned's former home in Old Barrack-lane; no one was to molest me; and the result of my repose, or what not, was to be communicated to Aletasters' Fraternity.

Well, the dreaded night arrived. There I was, undressed and in bed, waiting for the witching hour, cold and timid, but not trembling.

All was silent; the pale moon peered through the dirty window and I was restless, anxious for sleep, but with a heart (and pluck, too, I hoped) for any fate.

But hark!-a sound upon the stairs? Palpitation increased rapidly in my now troubled breast, and I began to tremble.

Yes, there was a slight rumbling noise from without. The dead silence continued for a minute. Raising myself partly, and resting upon my left arm, I prepared to resist material interference, when suddenly the chamber door opened, and in glided a tall figure draped in white!

Alas, for me! Friendless, helpless, terrified, I was ready to plead for mercy and freely surrender myself to the inevitable. In breathless suspense I gazed at the apparition. He beckoned me. He spoke not, for evidently he had nothing to say, or dared not speak. Still and watchful I remained. Then, in a moment came relief to my fluttering heart. The ghostly figure gave an un-ghostlike little peffin cough, which he could not conceal. This was sufficient evidence of materiality for me, and he seemed anxious to retreat! Beckoning me again, he stepped backward.

Out of bed I jumped and stood before him, like the fool that I was. Beckoning me again, he retired down the stairs with elephantine lightness. Now was my opportunity for satisfaction. 'Hang it! I'll see where tha cum from, and where tha'rt off to!' said I to myself, and, undressed though I was, I scampered after him. Out of doors and on Barrack-lane he went; I was after him, for I wasn't bound to nesh it at that critical moment; then on Langsett-road he ran, looking behind him in fear lest I should overtake and thrash him; on, on, we went, till I put out my arm to clutch him; when-Oh! My back! Oh, my ribs! – I had run against the stoops at the toll-bar, and was sprattling on the road!

'But did all this take place, Jacob, lad?' asked the chairman.

Yes, figuratively, I said. It was a dream! I'd tumbled out o'bed and hurt myself! The ghost escaped because I awoke in pain!

'But where does t'moral come in, Jacob, lad?'

Why, here, my friends. Never eat cold suet puddin' late at nights – leastways, not aboon a pound apiece – and then, happen, you'll not sleep in haunted houses!

Illustration from
A Christmas
Carol
British Library

By the close of the Victorian era reading ghost stories around a blazing fire on Christmas Eve had joined eating plum puddings and decorating the tree as a Yuletide tradition

A DRONFIELD GHOST STORY

By the close of the Victorian era reading ghost stories around a blazing fire on Christmas Eve had joined eating plum puddings and decorating the tree as a Yuletide tradition. Although Dickens' *A Christmas Carol* had popularised the ghost story for Christmas, the undoubted master of the genre was the Cambridge academic M.R. James. He was born during the reign of Queen Victoria but his best known stories, such as *A Warning to the Curious* and *Casting the Runes*, were published during the Edwardian period. James's ghosts were not the headless Elizabethan ladies or phantoms rattling chains found in the popular literature of the period. They were inexplicable, elemental creatures, unseen horrors that plagued individuals but were usually only glimpsed out of the corner of the eye. They could not be appeased or rationally explained. They just were.

The subtle change in the way ghost experiences were told is illustrated by a bone-chilling ghost story published by *The Sheffield Telegraph* on Christmas Eve, 1906. It tells of a phantom that haunted a house in one of the city's new suburbs.

'.....A young Sheffield couple recently married. They went to live at Dronfield. In the cellar of their house was a mysterious hole. It looked deep and dark, and was quite uncovered. They were curious about this hole, and ascertained that it was an old disused well, over which the house had been built. Why the house had been built over an old well, why the well had never been filled in, and why the hole had always been left uncovered, we cannot say....

But at all events there was the deep, dark, dismal well down in the cellar without so much as a board over it. The young wife never visited the cellar without a creepy sort of feeling. She always kept as far from the open well as she could, and nothing would induce her to open the cellar door after dark.

The cellar was, therefore, the most interesting thing in this Dronfield house which this young married Sheffield couple went out to occupy.

All went well for a time.

Then one night something happened. Two little girls belonging to Sheffield friends went out to Dronfield to spend the day, and they remained there to sleep. The young married couple had not fitted up all the bedrooms with beds, and so the young husband slept downstairs on the sofa, in the room over the cellar. The young wife and the children slept together upstairs.

Suddenly, in the darkness of the night, the young wife awoke.Suddenly, at the self-same moment, entirely unknown to her, the young husband, sleeping alone on the uncomfortable sofa over the cellar, also awoke. She heard footsteps on the stairs. They approached her room.

Scarcely daring to breathe, she did not cover her head in the bed clothes, but she daringly listened. The steps came nearer. The stairs creaked. The steps passed the door of her room and entered another bedroom. She breathed freely now. She thought it was her husband fetching another blanket for the sofa bed. Presently the steps, steadily, soberly returned and went down the stairs again. She did not speak, as she feared to disturb the children.

The footsteps were also heard by the husband – lying uneasily on the sofa.

He thought his wife was fetching something from the kitchen for the children; and he pulled himself together on the sofa and dozed off to sleep again.

At breakfast he asked her what she was doing downstairs in the night. Then they ascertained that neither had got out of bed, and that both had heard the steady steps on the stairs.

There was one corner of the room over the cellar in which they constantly heard, especially late at night, strange, mysterious knockings...

This was the first experience they had of the Dronfield ghost, for they were firmly convinced that what they had heard was the tread of some restless, departed occupant of the house, who knew more about the hole in the cellar than they did.

After that the ghost was always at work. Having been heard once, he apparently did not mind. There was one corner of the room over the cellar in which they constantly heard, especially late at night, strange mysterious knockings. The sounds came slow and muffled, as though someone was inside the wall and was patiently, persistently trying to hammer a way out. But the ghost was either weary from long working, or knew it was useless to try to hurry.

There was no eager impatience about the blows. They came as steadily and regularly as though they were being given by an arm that had grown old in the knocking. But the muffled sound went on night after night and refused to allow itself to be solved.

The young couple were greatly alarmed. They never slept without leaving a light burning. The light, they thought, would be a protection against the ghost if it came walking again. The real, old-fashioned ghosts, we believe, always had an objection to light.

But one night, not many nights ago, the young wife woke in great alarm.

The light was out.

It was terrible. She would have screamed if she could. But she felt powerless. She could not even rouse her husband. All the strength seemed to have gone out of her. She was certain someone was in the room, and had just extinguished the light.

She endured the uncertainty and the suspense as long as she could, and then, with feelings of almost desperation she sprang out of bed, seized the matches on the dressing-table, and struck a light. As the feeble light of the match illuminated the room she looked round, and there, looking her full in the face and pointing towards her, was a ghost. Spell-bound, she watched it until the match flickered out in her fingers. It was over in the corner, not far from the door – a hideous, ghostly sight.

It was a skeleton, and yet the fleshless bones seemed animated with life. The ugly eye-sockets appeared to see. She could not take her eyes off them. She was held with a speechless terror.

As the match burnt itself down, the apparition silently, stately, steadily, turned to go. Then all was dark again and she flung herself on the bed almost in a state of hysteria. The young husband, alarmed, sprang up in bed, gathered what had happened, and lit the gas. But the ghost had gone.

They did not sleep in the house again. As quickly as they could, they found another house, and they look back upon their horrifying experience at the house with the hole in the cellar with dread and alarm.

No satisfactory explanation is forthcoming.'

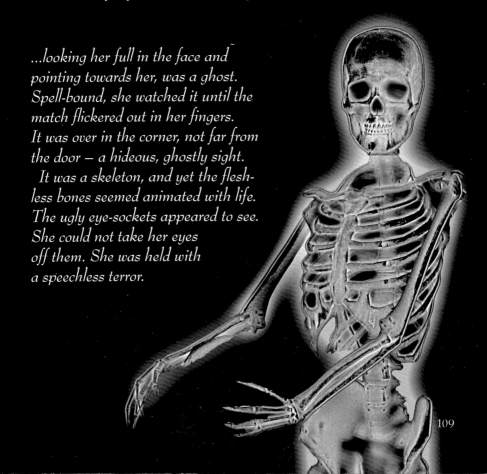

...looking her full in the face and pointing towards her, was a ghost. Spell-bound, she watched it until the match flickered out in her fingers. It was over in the corner, not far from the door – a hideous, ghostly sight.

It was a skeleton, and yet the flesh-less bones seemed animated with life. The ugly eye-sockets appeared to see. She could not take her eyes off them. She was held with a speechless terror.

109

Bibliography

Addy, Sidney Oldall (1888). *A Glossary of Words used in the neighbour-hood of Sheffield.*

(1893)*The Hall of Waltheof, or the Early Condition and settlement of Hallamshire.* Sheffield.

(1895) *Household Tales with other Traditional Remains.* Sheffield.

Bean, J.P. (1987). *Crime in Sheffield.* Sheffield City Libraries.

Bell, Karl (2012). *The Legend of Spring-heeled Jack.* Woodbridge: Boydell Press.

Clarke, David (1993). *Strange South Yorkshire: Myth and Magic in the Valley of the Don.* Wilmslow: Sigma.

Clarke, Roger (2012). *A Natural History of Ghosts.* London: Penguin.

Davies, Owen (2007). *The Haunted: A Social History of Ghosts.* Basingstoke: Palgrave.

Gatty, Alfred (1884). *A Life at One Living.* London: Bell & Sons.

Haining, Peter (1992). *Charles Dickens' Xmas Christmas Ghost Stories.* London: Robert Hale.

(1977). *The Legend and Bizarre Crimes of Spring-heeled Jack.* London: Muller.

Harrison, Samuel (1864). *A Complete History of the Great Flood at Sheffield.* Sheffield.

Hunter, Joseph (1829). *The Hallamshire Glossary.* Sheffield.

Kingston, J. & Smaridge, M. (1980). *Henry Tatton's Notebook.* Sheffield City Libraries.

Machan, Peter (2004). *Sheffield's Time Trail: True Tales from the Norfolk Heritage Trail.* Sheffield: Green Estate.

Reade, Charles (1870). *Put Yourself in His Place.* London.

Salim, Valerie (1983). *Ghost Hunter's Guide to Sheffield.* Sheffield: Sheaf.

(1987). *More Sheffield Ghosts & where to find them.* Sheffield: Sheaf.

Sharpe, James (2005). *Dick Turpin: The Myth of the English Highwayman.* London: Profile.

Vickers, J. Edward (1972). *Old Sheffield Town.* Wakefield: EP.

(1978). *A Popular History of Sheffield.* Wakefield: EP.

Woolhouse, Joseph (1832). *A description of the town of Sheffield.* Sheffield.